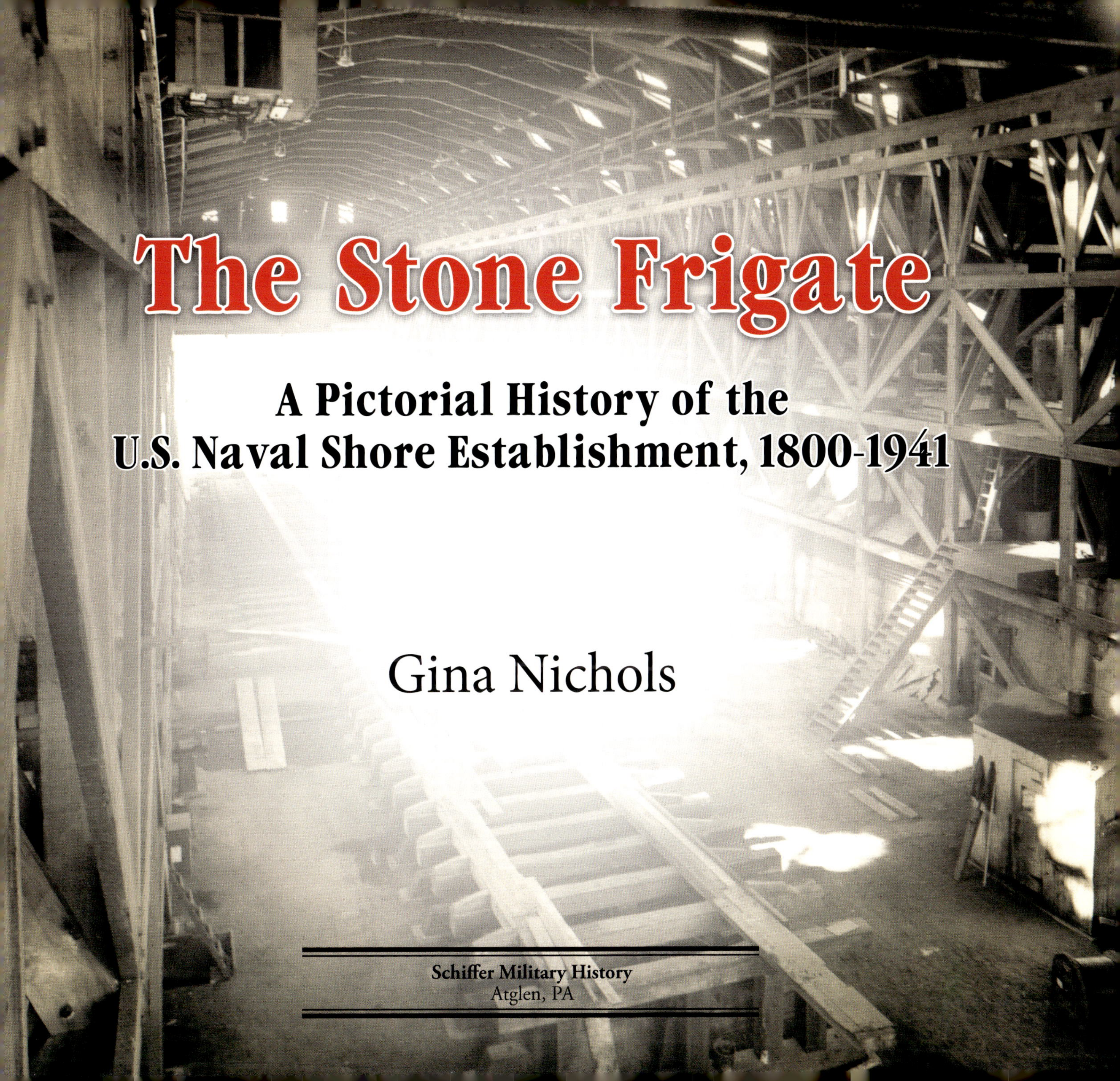

The Stone Frigate

A Pictorial History of the U.S. Naval Shore Establishment, 1800-1941

Gina Nichols

Schiffer Military History
Atglen, PA

Acknowledgments

First and most importantly, thank you to my son, Hunter, for all his patience and support. Special thanks to Robert Quinn, Kimberlyn Crowell, Kevin Hughes, Tim Buckley, Bill Shaner, and Don Turner, who let me pick their brains and read parts or all of several drafts with invaluable suggestions. Thank you for all your assistance, patience, and most of all, your time. Thank you, Ben, for honoring me by writing the foreword for my book.

Much of the research for this book took place at the U.S. Navy Seabee Museum Archives, the Library of Congress, National Archives, and the Naval History and Heritage Center Photographic Collection. Their amazing, unique, and varied collections and archival materials helped to make this book possible. Thank you all for all the hard work you do and your contributions to preserving history.

Library of Congress Control Number: 2013939684

Book design by Mark David Bowyer.

Printed in China
ISBN: 978-0-7643-4339-1

We are interested in hearing from authors with book ideas on related topics.

Published by Schiffer Publishing Ltd.
4880 Lower Valley Road
Atglen, PA 19310
Phone: (610) 593-1777
FAX: (610) 593-2002
E-mail: Info@schifferbooks.com.
Visit our web site at: **www.schifferbooks.com**
Please write for a free catalog.
This book may be purchased from the publisher.
Try your bookstore first.

Contents

Foreword

The history of every nation is influenced by many factors: culture, geography, commerce, and the migration patterns of people, among others. A common factor among the planet's great nations has been the need to defend their territory from those who would attempt to usurp it.

This was true of the newest of the soon to be global power, the United States of America, from its birth until the present. The infrastructure and systems to defend this growing nation would be dictated by its unique geography. Beyond its northern and southern borders, it faced the world from the shores of two great oceans and the Gulf of Mexico. Though a blessing for commerce, it also presented a formidable task to defend the nation from aggressors.

This necessitated the requirement to become a maritime power to protect commercial sea lanes around the globe and the homeland. The nation's history is replete with the names of ships and men who fulfilled this mission heroically.

This treatise brings to life and documents the accomplishments of the lesser-known men and women who planned, designed, built, and maintained the shore establishment which provided the vital support required by a great navy. The author's research has produced a vivid view of one slice of the growth of the United States. The photographs speak to the skills of engineers and craftsmen, both military and civilian, who built the tailored structures and facilities which to this day dot the coastlines and interior of the country.

Those who serve or have served in the latter day Civil Engineer Corps, the Seabees, or the Naval Facilities Engineering Command enjoy a proud legacy created by the Bureau of Yards and Docks and those early engineers and Seabees.

—Rear Admiral Benjamin Montoya, CEC, USN (ret.)
Chairman, CEC/Seabee Historical Foundation
Former Commander, Naval Facilities Engineering Command
and Chief of the Civil Engineer Corps

Introduction

The British Royal Navy coined the term *Stone Frigate* to describe their first naval shore establishment. The Royal Navy first used the term in 1805 when they chose Diamond Rock, off Martinique, as a strategic home port from which to harass the French Navy and French merchant ships in the Caribbean while blocking the approach to Martinique. Commodore Samuel Hood chose Lieutenant James Wilkes Maurice as the first commander of the Stone Frigate. Wilkes operated the site with a crew of 120 men and just one canon taken from Commodore Hood's ship until the French captured it in the Battle of Diamond Rock later that year.

Until the late nineteenth century, the Royal Navy housed, trained, and supported their fleet from old wooden ships of the line. The Royal Navy moored these ships at ports and used them as receiving ships, barracks, and depots to keep costs down and maintain discipline. As ships began to use more increasingly complex technology during the late nineteenth century, these ship facilities became too large to continue afloat, and they moved to shore establishments while keeping the name Stone Frigate. The U.S. Navy began with much the same approach. However, its first Secretary of the Navy, Benjamin Stoddert, realized in 1798 the advantages of a shore establishment, and requested funds for the first six navy yards. The *Stone Frigate* is a pictorial account of the activities of personnel, machines, and equipment used in the creation, development, and evolution of the U.S. naval shore establishment from 1800 to 1941.

Chapter 1: The Stone Frigate

Colored lithograph shows the Washington Navy Yard waterfront, published by E. Sachse & Company, Baltimore, Maryland, c. 1862. The lithograph illustrates the Washington Navy Yard as seen from above the Anacostia River, with Building 1, the Commandant's House, and the trophy gun park in the center. *Courtesy of the Naval History and Heritage Command.*

Test of the U.S. Crane Ship *Kearsarge's* 250-ton revolving crane at the Philadelphia Navy Yard, Pennsylvania, October 27, 1922. On August 29, 1919, the USS *Kearsarge* moved to the Philadelphia Navy Yard, where she decommissioned and converted to a crane ship. The Navy added an enormous 250-ton capacity revolving crane to the *Kearsarge*, as well as anti-torpedo hull "blisters" to stabilize her. *Courtesy of the Naval History and Heritage Command.*

The Navy's transition from nineteenth century wooden sailing vessels to the nuclear carriers, cruisers, and submarines of today influenced and shaped today's naval facilities. As major technological, military, and political events of the past transpired, the shore establishment infrastructure expanded and developed in order to support fleet requirements and sustain the Navy. The history of the naval shore establishment conveys how a few nineteenth century navy yards expanded into a global system of naval stations, supply depots, air stations, and bases.

Naval shore establishments encompass a large number of separate and varied facilities, ranging from early small radio-compass stations to today's large air stations, shipyards, and bases. Today's shore facilities descended from the original six yards designed to build ships and support fleet activities. In order to preserve the yards, the Navy designed a system of public works that expanded from maintaining a pier with a few warehouses, to include the care and upkeep of all transportation, utilities, ship facilities, and structures. As naval technology advanced, public works evolved to support the new hi-tech Navy.

The USS *Delaware* entering Dry Dock Number 1 at Gosport (Norfolk) Navy Yard, Portsmouth, Virginia, June 17, 1833. The festivities celebrated the first dry-docking of a ship on the U.S. East Coast. Although not completed, Commodore Lewis Warrington ordered the *Delaware* pulled in for repairs, in order to beat the almost completed Navy dry dock in Charlestown, Massachusetts. Except for a brief time during the Civil War, Dry Dock Number 1 at Norfolk has continued to maintain operational status since its christening. The Norfolk Navy Yard experienced tremendous improvements in the mid-nineteenth century. In 1845 a new building slip began, and in August 1846, the Navy purchased the lot on the north side of the navy yard, known as Saint Helena. The Bureau of Yards and Docks constructed storehouses, a blacksmith shop, and heavy apparatus turning machine, foundry, and plumbing shop for the base. In 1848, they completed a quay wall and a cofferdam began. On the newly acquired Fort Norfolk land transferred from the War Department the Navy built new magazines. In 1855, the Navy installed gas works for lighting the yards and buildings. All of these improvements and more made the Norfolk Navy Yard one of the best-equipped and prepared Navy yards at the time. *Courtesy of the Naval History and Heritage Command.*

The emerging nation initially created the Continental Navy on June 12, 1775, to protect shipping, defend coastal cities, and gain foreign support. However, by 1787, with the treasury empty and a huge war debt, the nation could no longer afford a standing Navy, and sold the last of its armed vessels. Unfortunately, peaceful isolation did not last long for the United States. In 1785, the Algerian Barbary States commenced preying upon U.S. merchant ships. By 1793, increasing difficulties between the United States and Algiers erupted after a series of peace treaties between Algiers, Spain, and Portugal opened the Straits of Gibraltar to Barbary Corsair pirates. Shortly thereafter, the Corsairs captured 13 American vessels and 119 American merchantmen. In response Congress passed the 1794 Naval Act, authorizing the construction of six frigates and the formation of a preliminary naval establishment under the supervision of the Secretary of War.

Work on the frigates began under the direction of Secretary of War Henry Knox, who handled all marine matters. The Navy chose the ports of Charlestown (Boston), Massachusetts; New York, New York; Philadelphia, Pennsylvania; Baltimore, Maryland; Gosport (Norfolk),

Portrait of British-born architect Benjamin Latrobe. Best known for his design of the United States Capitol, Latrobe came to the United States in 1796. In 1803, the U.S. hired Latrobe as Surveyor for the Public Buildings of the United States, and he spent the next fourteen years working on projects in Washington, D.C. In 1820, while in New Orleans working on a waterworks project, Latrobe died from yellow fever. Portrait painted by Charles Willson Peale, c. 1804. *Courtesy of the U.S. Navy Seabee Museum.*

Virginia; and Portsmouth, New Hampshire, to each construct a ship because of their shipbuilding history, as well as to distribute the financial advantages arising from the operation.

At the close of 1795, while the ships were still under construction, diplomatic dialogue with Algiers resulted in a humiliating treaty. The United States agreed to pay an annual tribute to the pirates in exchange for releasing American prisoners and ceasing all future attacks on American merchantmen. Although the peace agreement between the United States and the Regency of Algiers required the U.S. to cease all shipbuilding, Congress authorized completion of three of the original six frigates. The *United States* launched July 10, 1797, at Philadelphia; the *Constellation* on September 7, 1797, at Baltimore; and the *Constitution* on September 20, 1797, at Boston.

In 1798, after the quasi-war with France resulted in the capture of approximately 308 American merchantmen, Congress authorized the construction, purchase, or hire of twelve armed vessels. On April 30, 1798, Congress removed jurisdiction of all naval affairs from the Secretary of War and authorized the Navy Department be established. Benjamin Stoddert's first concern, after appointment as the first Secretary of the Navy, was the construction and outfitting of ships. However, after studying the prior outsourcing of shipbuilding in 1794 and realizing its excessive cost, Stoddert believed it was essential that the Navy maintain and operate its own shipbuilding yards and facilities.

View of the parade grounds and quarters at the Pensacola Navy Yard, August 15, 1888. On the right is a small frame building used as a scale house for coal. In 1824, Secretary of the Navy Samuel Southard recommended a site be chosen on the Florida coast for establishing a navy yard in order to protect the newly established states along the Gulf Coast. The Navy chose Tartar's Point on Pensacola Bay after realizing the advantages of the harbor and observing the large timber reserves that neighbored the land for shipbuilding. Sparsely settled and containing almost no labor force within a reasonable distance of the facility, for many years it remained necessary to import expert laborers from the north. By 1836 the Navy recognized the Pensacola Navy Yard's importance, and they established a commission to make a full and complete master plan for developing the yard into a first class station. For decades the Navy made generous appropriations towards the base, which, by the beginning of the Civil War, made it one of the best-equipped stations in the shore establishment. *Courtesy of the Naval History and Heritage Command.*

View of the first marine railway at the Washington Navy Yard, July 23, 1920. In 1822, Commodore John Rodgers designed and built the first marine railway at the Washington Navy Yard in 1823. This was the first marine railway constructed and installed in the United States. *Courtesy of the U.S. Navy Seabee Museum.*

On February 25, 1799, Congress passed an act to appropriate $1.2 million for the construction of six 74-gun ships, the building of two docks, and the purchase of timber and timberlands for future use by the Navy. No funds had been appropriated for the purchase of land, but the sum was $50,000 more than requested, which encouraged Secretary Stoddert to purchase property for the much needed shore bases.

Stoddert purchased property in or near five of the cities chosen for building the original six frigates – Portsmouth, New Hampshire; Charlestown, Massachusetts; New York, New York; Philadelphia, Pennsylvania; and Gosport, Virginia – and the sixth site chosen was the new capital of Washington. Stoddert had little difficulty deciding that the proper course to pursue incorporated making the yards at Norfolk, Washington, New York, and Portsmouth public property and permanent. In 1801, Stoddert requested an additional $500,000 from Congress to complete the frigates and finish constructing navy yards, docks, and wharves.

However, the day after President Jefferson assumed office in 1801, he sought enactment of a law to provide for a peace establishment.

Commodore Lewis Warrington, the first Chief of the Bureau of Navy Yards and Docks. From 1826 to 1830, Commodore Warrington served as one of the three Navy Board commissioners, a body charged with the administration of naval affairs. Afterwards, Warrington returned to the Norfolk Navy Yard to serve as commandant. In 1840, the Navy reassigned him to Washington to serve for another two years as commissioner on the Navy Board. After the Navy reorganized the department in 1842, Warrington became the first Chief of the Bureau of Navy Yards and Docks. On February 28, 1844, Secretary of the Navy Thomas W. Gilmer died of wounds received after the large cannon "Peacemaker" exploded during a firing demonstration on board the USS *Princeton*. Warrington served as interim Secretary of the Navy for one month afterwards. In 1846 Warrington became Chief of the Bureau of Ordnance, an office he held until his death on October 12, 1851. *Courtesy of the U.S. Navy Seabee Museum.*

The Bureau of Yards and Docks logo, created c. 1862. In 1862, Congress approved extending the Navy Department bureau system by amending the titles of three of the existing bureaus and adding three additional bureaus. The only modification to the Bureau of Navy Yards and Docks was a shortening of its name to the Bureau of Yards and Docks. *Courtesy of the U.S. Navy Seabee Museum.*

General view of the Boston Navy Yard and Dry Dock Number 2 from the east, April 20, 1899. In 1899, work began on the new granite and concrete dry dock, the largest dry dock of its type built at that time. The dry dock cost $1.25 million to construct, was 800 feet long, and 112 feet wide. *Courtesy of U.S. Navy Seabee Museum.*

As a result, Jefferson was able to effect a great reduction of the Navy, and discharged all naval officers except 9 captains, 36 lieutenants, 150 midshipmen, and 1,200 seamen. The plan also included selling all ships except thirteen frigates, of which only six were kept in commission and the rest were mothballed. A large portion of the $500,000 appropriated for Navy yard construction and improvements was ordered returned to the Treasury unspent.

To preserve the mothballed fleet, Jefferson appointed Benjamin Latrobe, the Navy's first civil engineer, to submit plans for a dry dock capable of holding twelve 44-gun frigates at the Washington Navy Yard. Latrobe submitted the plans, but Congress failed to appropriate the funds, and the dry dock was never built. However, Jefferson, interested in investing in the new capital city, was eager to invest in the yard by making it the main naval repair facility and chief storage area for naval supplies.

View of the Memphis Navy Yard from the Arkansas shore, c. 1852. Drawing from *Gleason's Pictorial Drawing Room Companion*. One of the first problems the new Bureau of Navy Yards and Docks faced included the proposal to construct another navy yard in the nation's interior. The early shore establishment grew extremely slowly. By 1842, the Navy had added little to the naval shore establishment except for a seventh navy yard in Pensacola, Florida. The invention of steam transportation inspired those living near large inland waterways in the nation's interior to become interested in naval defense. The Tennessee legislature proposed the establishment of a naval base in Memphis to the Congressional Naval Affairs Committee. In 1843, a board of three naval officers was appointed to examine and survey the harbor of Memphis to observe its capability as a naval depot and yard in order to build and repair steam ships and other vessels of war. In 1844, the same three naval officers and Civil Engineer W.P.S. Sanger returned to Memphis to select a site for the yard. Although the Navy allocated considerable funds towards land acquisition and station construction, after several years the high level of erosion difficulties and unstable soil conditions caused an investigative board to recommend closure of the yard in 1852. In 1854, Congress approved ceding the land and all materiel and equipment to the City of Memphis. *Courtesy of the Naval History and Heritage Command.*

Jefferson designated Latrobe "Engineer of the Navy Department" in 1804, and ordered him to submit a master plan for the Washington Navy Yard. After completing the master plan, Latrobe continued his connection with the Navy by designing a gate house, three building slips, and Quarters "A" and "B" at the Washington Navy Yard. Latrobe also prepared designs, estimates, and reports for buildings at the New York and Norfolk yards.

The naval war on the Great Lakes from 1812-1814 compelled the Navy to build yards and naval stations on Lakes Ontario, Erie, and Champlain. While Congress had authorized the establishment of three dockyards, nothing more than the surveys and reports had been completed by the end of the war. However, three naval stations at Sackett's Harbor, New York; Erie, Pennsylvania; and Whitehall, Michigan, were completed. Although these stations were very active during the War of 1812, they fell into decay in the postwar years, and the Erie and Whitehall stations were disestablished. By the middle of 1825 the base at Sackett's Harbor was greatly reduced, and only a handful of men and two ships remained to guard the Canadian border.

In February 1815, seventeen years after the establishment of the position of Secretary of the Navy, the Navy Department authorized the formation of a Board of Commissioners to relieve the Secretary of some responsibilities related to the civilian functions of the Navy. The Board, composed of three post-captains, discharged all official duties of the Navy office related to procurement of naval stores and materials and the construction, armament, equipment, and employment of vessels of war, as well as all other matters connected with the naval establishment.

Bay State Dredging Company of Boston dredges Dry Dock Number 2 at the Boston Navy Yard on June 1, 1899. On August 12, 1905, Dry Dock Number 2 began operating after the USS *Maryland* docked. *Courtesy of the U.S. Navy Seabee Museum.*

View of the Portsmouth Navy Yard, Maine, c. 1853 from across the bay. Although named for the city of Portsmouth, New Hampshire, the Portsmouth Navy Yard is located on Seavey's Island, across the Piscataqua River in Kittery, Maine. Sketch from *Gleason's Pictorial Drawing Room Companion*, published in 1853 in Boston, Massachusetts. At the left is the Franklin Shiphouse, completed in 1838 and lengthened in 1854, making it one of the largest in the country at the time. In the mid-1850s, the Portsmouth Navy Yard underwent a significant amount of construction, including a powder magazine, a timber shed, commander's quarters, brick stables, lime house, coal house, and watchman's quarters. The Navy ordered machinery and tools for a smithery shortly after the cooper's shop was completed. A main project completed included the installation of a 1400-foot cylindrical brick and cement covered sewer with a cistern designed to carry all waste water to the tide. *Courtesy of the Naval History and Heritage Command.*

View of the Norfolk Navy Yard after both the Confederate and Union Armies destroyed it during the Civil War, December 1864. The yard burned twice during the Civil War, and by the end of the war was in a seriously weakened status. The yard destruction included nearly all land structures, except for the officer's quarters. Dry Dock Number 1 survived, although both the Confederate and Union Armies each blew up the gates on their way out of the yard. In addition machines, ships' masts, and timber were strewn about the yard when the Union re-entered the yard in April 1861. *Courtesy of the National Archives.*

Artist rendering of the USS *Merrimack* and the Norfolk Navy Yard destruction during the Civil War, April 1861. Commodore Hiram Paulding, instructed to destroy crucial military materiel rather than leave them for Confederate troops, ordered the destruction of the Norfolk Navy Yard and nearby ships. *Courtesy of the Naval History and Heritage Command.*

Once Spain ceded Florida to the United States in 1819, the Navy began looking for a suitable location for a new Navy yard on the Gulf Coast. Realizing the advantages of Pensacola harbor and the large timber reserves nearby for shipbuilding, they chose Tartar's Point on Pensacola Bay in 1826 to become the seventh Navy yard. In addition to the original six navy yards and the new Pensacola Navy Yard, the naval shore establishment of the 1820s included naval stations, recruiting stations, and naval hospitals.

The Board of Commissioners convinced Congress in 1825 that the country needed dry docks to repair ships, frigates, and small vessels. Secretary Samuel Southard recommended the erection of two dry docks, one each at Boston and Norfolk. Although many structures were built at the yards, until this time no organized plans were made for the growth and improvement of any installation besides the Washington Navy Yard. To remedy this, Congress enacted a law directing navy yards be thoroughly examined and plans prepared for their improvement and preservation. The Board of Commissioners hired Loammi Baldwin as a consulting engineer to examine the various navy yards and form potential plans for their improvement.

Based on Baldwin's surveys and estimates, the dry docks at the Boston and Norfolk yards began construction in 1827. Because of the distance between Boston and Norfolk, Baldwin appointed engineers Alexander Parris and William P.S. Sanger, respectively, to represent him at each yard. From 1827 to 1834, Baldwin also surveyed the New York Navy Yard to determine the best location for a dry dock.

Three major innovations – steam power, marine railways, and the shiphouse – changed the tone of the Navy's shipyards during the first half of the nineteenth century. While steam was not yet used to propel naval vessels, it was used in the operation of labor saving machinery at the navy yards as early as 1805. By 1830, steam was a major propellant at the Washington Navy Yard, powering saw gates, circular saws, hydraulic bellows, forging hammers, turning and boring lathes, and grindstones.

The marine railway became the first advanced technique developed to haul a ship out of water to allow extensive work on the hull. Before this time, men hauled ships needing hull repairs on shore at high tide and careened them on their sides to expose half of the hull at a time. This new invention eased repairs and sped removal to and from the water. Marine railways became indispensable at any navy yard or installation around the world.

The third major innovation was the shiphouse, huge hangar-like covered structures that provided shelter for ships during their overhauls, or when laid up "in ordinary." Engineers first suggested shiphouses be constructed over the ship's ways at Boston and Portsmouth, not only to protect the workers from the elements, but also to increase work speed and efficiency. Shiphouses also protected the vessels themselves from any material deterioration.

USS *Amphitrite* in dry dock while stationed at the Port Royal Navy Yard c. 1895-96. At their yard in Wilmington, Delaware, Harlan and Hollingsworth laid down the second USS *Amphitrite* in 1874. She was the lead ship in her class of iron-hulled, twin-screw monitors, and launched on June 7, 1883. The Navy did not commission her until April 23, 1895, due to rapid changes in naval technology and doctrine that repeatedly delayed her progress, causing her to be redesigned twice while still under construction. *Courtesy of the U.S. Navy Seabee Museum.*

Photograph of the first dry dock at the Philadelphia Navy Yard, League Island, Pennsylvania, c. 1891. Robert Peary, Civil Engineer Corps officer and noted arctic explorer, designed the 500-foot Dry Dock Number 1. The dry dock was completed in 1891. *Courtesy of the U.S. Navy Seabee Museum.*

View of the main portion of New London Submarine Base from Building 3 looking south, July 2, 1928. In 1868, the Navy established a coaling station at New London, Connecticut, on an eighty-acre site on the east bank of the Thames River. Initial construction at the station included storehouses, offices, pump room, watch house, quarter's buildings, and a stable. The New London Naval Station was recommissioned the first continental submarine base in December 1915. During the construction program of World War I eight finger piers were built, together with storehouses, shops, and barracks, raising the number of buildings on the base to forty-three. *Courtesy of the U.S. Navy Seabee Museum.*

By 1842 naval administrative duties had expanded significantly, necessitating a system be established under the Secretary of the Navy. On August 31, 1842, naval leadership created a Bureau system to replace the Board of Naval Commissioners. The five new Bureaus included the Bureau of Navy Yards and Docks; the Bureau of Construction, Equipment, and Repair; the Bureau of Provisions and Clothing; the Bureau of Ordnance and Hydrography; and the Bureau of Medicine and Surgery.

Congress granted to the Secretary of the Navy the right to assign and distribute among the Bureaus the duties of the Navy Department as he saw fit to accomplish its duties. Each Bureau performed its duties under the authority of the Secretary of the Navy, and its orders were considered as emanating from him, giving them the full force and effect of his authority.

President John Tyler immediately put the Bureau system into operation and appointed Commodore Lewis Warrington, then president of the Board of Navy Commissioners, to be the first Chief of the Bureau of Navy Yards and Docks. The Bureau was vested with the construction and maintenance of the docks, wharves, and buildings within the navy yards. In addition to Warrington and Chief Engineer Sanger, the personnel of the Bureau in 1842 consisted of only a chief clerk, two clerks, a draftsman, and a messenger.

The twenty-year period between the creation of the Bureau of Navy Yards and Docks and the Civil War was a period of tremendous growth for the naval shore establishment. In 1844, the invention of steam transportation brought about the establishment of the Memphis Naval Station in Tennessee to defend Americans living in the nation's interior near large inland waterways. Most of the navy yards underwent essential construction to maintain the buildings and keep up with new industrial inventions, including gas works, railroads, and steam driven tools. The strategic value of the Pensacola Navy Yard also warranted the Navy to designate significant appropriations towards base improvements. In order to help the yard become a center for shipbuilding in the South, a graving dock and the essential shops and plants were built.

Coal shed at the New London Naval Station in 1915 prior to being redesignated a submarine base. In 1898, the yard was converted into a coaling station for small warships. These ships were given their fuel from the coal shed and coal dump until another more advance coaling mechanism and shed could be constructed. *Courtesy of the U.S. Navy Seabee Museum.*

Rear Admiral Mordecai T. Endicott

On April 7, 1898, President William McKinley broke precedence and appointed Mordecai Endicott to become the first member of the Civil Engineer Corps to command the Bureau of Yards and Docks. He was immediately elevated to the rank of Commodore, and later Rear Admiral. Endicott became the first Chief to hold the rank of Rear Admiral, one which has been held by all Chiefs of the Bureau ever since. He was reappointed Chief in 1902 and again in 1906. Born in May's Landing, New Jersey, on November 26, 1844, Endicott attended private and parochial schools, as well as private tutoring for his early education. He graduated from Rensselaer Polytechnic Institute with a civil engineering degree in 1869. In 1871, he was selected assistant civil engineer at the League Island Naval Station, Philadelphia. Commissioned into the Naval Civil Engineer Corps on July 13, 1874, Endicott spent the next 16 years serving at various east coast navy yards. In 1890 he served as a consulting engineer in Washington, D.C., and was given virtual control of all civil engineering projects. At this time most of the navy yards underwent extensive modernization, which allowed Endicott to show his exceptional professional talent and vision. Thus, Endicott played a significant part in the introduction of electrical equipment and implementing the use of steel and concrete dry docks instead of the old timbered structures. One of his most significant achievements was the completion of the floating dry dock DEWEY, the largest of its type built at the time. From 1905 to 1907, Endicott also served on the Panama Canal Commission. He was chosen for this service because of his role on the 1895 Nicaragua Canal Commission to study the feasibility of building a canal there. Endicott resigned as Chief in 1907, but continued on active duty for several months until appointed as technical advisor to the Justice Department. He retired in 1909, but returned to duty as a Justice Department technical advisor from 1914 to 1917. Endicott later aided the Bureau of Yards and Docks during the World War I wartime effort. Endicott passed away at his home on March 5, 1926, and was buried in Arlington National Cemetery. *Courtesy of the U.S. Navy Seabee Museum.*

The USS *Peoria* perched in the Key West Naval Station's marine railway, July 28, 1913. Completed July 24, 1911, the marine railway operated via a steam engine and endless chain-haul. The chain acted over double wildcats at the engine and double sheave outhaul blocks secured to the track near the outboard end. It led to two idler sheaves, one near the front of the cradle and one near the center. The latter was for the down haul section of chain. *Courtesy of the U.S. Navy Seabee Museum.*

The settlement of differences with Great Britain over Oregon, the acquisition of California and New Mexico, and the discovery of gold in California greatly enhanced the importance of the Pacific Squadron. As early as 1838, Secretary James Paulding recognized the need for a naval depot on the West Coast, and ordered the commander of the Pacific Squadron to make a close and accurate survey of the Straits of Juan de Fuca in order to ascertain their suitability for a naval station. Paulding also ordered Lt. Charles Wilkes to explore the coast between the Columbia River and the San Francisco Bay. In 1847, after Commodore John D. Sloat captured the Spanish base in Monterey, California, Secretary John Mason selected it as the newest Pacific coast naval station and established Naval Port Monterey. In 1848, after the Mexican-American War ended, a joint board of Army and Navy officers was organized to report on the locations of former Mexican owned fortifications, lighthouses, navy yards, and dry docks for future use as military bases.

With the admission of California as a state in 1850, a base for ship repair and supplies became necessary in order to maintain a squadron on the West Coast. A floating dry dock, built in the east and shipped to San Francisco in 1852, required a mooring place where it could service the fleet. In accordance with the authority of Congress, the Secretary of the Navy appointed a board in 1852 to choose a site near San Francisco Bay for a navy yard. The board selected Mare Island, situated some 30 miles north of San Francisco Bay. The Navy formally established the Mare Island Navy Yard in September 1854, with Commander David Farragut as its first commander.

In 1862, Congress approved an extension of the Navy Department Bureau system by means of amending the titles of three of the existing Bureaus and adding three additional Bureaus. The only modification to the Bureau of Navy Yards and Docks was a shortening of its name to the Bureau of Yards and Docks. However, the act did authorize an increase in the Bureau's civilian staff from five to eleven civilians to meet wartime conditions.

Despite the amazing strides accomplished towards expanding and improving the shore establishment prior to 1860, several major naval facilities were destroyed during the Civil War. On January 14, 1861, four days after Florida seceded from the Union, the Secretary of the Navy received a telegram from Captain James Armstrong, Commander of the Pensacola Navy Yard, stating that an armed commission, representing the Governor of Florida, had taken over the magazine and demanded surrender of the entire yard. The Confederates met no opposition upon entering the yard, despite the ample number of men and weaponry available. Captain Armstrong accepted the Confederate terms, and the Union lost one of the best-equipped navy yards in the country without any opposition.

Additionally, the Norfolk Navy Yard, one of the most highly developed naval installations in the United States, was lost to the Confederates in April 1861. At the time, the property was valued at $10 million dollars and was the worst loss sustained by the Navy during the Civil War. Besides the storehouses and a large number of dwellings, shops, storehouses, and provisions, the yard was well armed with thousands of firearms, including three hundred Dahlgren guns. Twelve ships were also anchored at the Norfolk yard at the time, including the USS *Merrimac*, which was undergoing repair work.

On April 10th, Secretary Gideon Welles advised Norfolk's Commandant, Charles Stewart McCauley, to prepare for an assault on the yard by the state militia which, while not yet members of the Confederacy, were reported to be seething with secessionist sentiment. The Bureau of Steam Engineering dispatched Chief Engineer Benjamin Isherwood to supervise the reassembling of the *Merrimac's* machinery in order to move her north out of danger. McCauley, afraid of provoking the militia due to Isherwood's activities, blocked Isherwood from reassembling the *Merrimac*.

Secretary Welles sent Commodore Paulding to relieve McCauley shortly after Virginia seceded with the order to evacuate or destroy all naval materials and shipping at Norfolk. Marines and enlisted personnel mined the dry dock and spread turpentine-soaked cotton and gunpowder around buildings and the top-hampers of the anchored vessels. Just prior to dawn on April 21, 1861, the men lit the powder trains, the Union retreated, and the entire yard went up in flames.

The yard remained in Confederate hands until May 1862, when the Confederate troops burned it once again as the Union Army approached. When the Union Army arrived, only five brick quarters, a boiler shop, a foundry, and one timber shed remained of the ten million dollar naval facility.

The Confederates also abandoned Pensacola in 1862, and the men found the yard in ruins. The Navy, realizing the strategic location and the need for a repair and supply depot in the South, commenced repairing the yard and rebuilding structures. They restored the facility, and it quickly began functioning as a repair center for the Gulf Blockading Squadron under the direction of Admiral David Farragut.

During the Civil War the northern navy yards served as depots, manufacturing workshops, and repair centers. Facilities improved and the workforce quadrupled. The New York Navy Yard became the Union's most important facility because of its access to artisans, laborers, and commodities, as well as its location. During the war the yard built sixteen ships, outfitted over four hundred merchant ships as armed cruisers, and repaired several hundred fighting ships.

Aerial photograph of the Key West Naval Station and post office, December 19, 1936. In 1908, the Navy constructed the Key West Naval Radio Station as an important link in the Navy's communication system at the naval station. In 1932, the Key West Naval Station was placed in caretaker status, and personnel operating the Navy Radio Station remained the defunct station's only occupants until 1939, when the threat of war in Europe called for the closed base to officially reopen. *Courtesy of the U.S. Navy Seabee Museum.*

Photograph of Dry Dock Number 4 at the New York Navy Yard, looking northeast towards the Williamsburg Bridge from Building 41, September 4, 1912. In 1900, Congress appropriated $1 million dollars for the construction of the granite and concrete dry dock originally set to be 554 feet long. By its completion in 1912, the dry dock had been redesigned to be 728 feet long and 120 feet wide, which made it possible to dock the largest Dreadnought in the fleet. *Courtesy of the U.S. Navy Seabee Museum.*

The Union naval forces also established a series of naval stations for maintenance and repair at Mound City, Illinois; Memphis, Tennessee; Port Royal and Beaufort, South Carolina; and Baltimore, Maryland, for the maintenance and repair of northern blockading and patrolling squadrons. These stations were well equipped with facilities for repairing vessels and storing ordnance, provisions, and coal. The Navy also established a niter depot, used to store niter – historically a major ingredient in gunpowder – at Malden, Massachusetts, in 1864.

The Civil War revolutionized methods of shipbuilding, and the encounters between the ironclads demonstrated the superiority of steam driven iron vessels over wooden sailing ships. However, this new breed of ship required construction at a new type of facility, with the foundries, shops, and docks adapted to the growing needs of the Navy. Two major shipyard requirements for ironclad construction included fresh water for the preservation of the iron vessels and security from attack by a foreign enemy. The Philadelphia area fulfilled both requirements.

Prior to this need, the original Philadelphia Navy Yard had declined in importance due to its confined acreage and interior location. The advantages of the Philadelphia area increased significantly when evaluated in terms of requirements for steam manufacture of iron ships, engines, and armaments. Philadelphia possessed all the natural advantages for an iron shipbuilding center, including being located in the country's principal iron and coal mining regions, its access to the fresh waters of the Delaware River, and its large skilled labor pool.

The city of Philadelphia offered the Navy 900 acres of marshland known as League Island for one dollar. On February 18, 1867, Congress authorized acceptance of title for League Island, but adequate funding to begin construction was not provided for another six years. The Pennsylvania Railroad Company purchased the old yard for the sum of one million dollars, of which the Navy used almost half to erect buildings, wharves, and causeways at League Island.

The new steam powered fleet also led to the establishment of the naval coaling station. By 1855, the increase in steam for ship propulsion raised the question of establishing coaling stations both at home and at key international locations. By 1857, the Navy appropriated funds for establishing a coal depot at Key West, Florida, and later another at Port Royal, South Carolina. In 1868, the Navy established a coaling station at New London, Connecticut, on an eighty-acre site on the east bank of the Thames River. Permanent coaling stations did not appear on foreign soil until 1878, when the Navy took steps to establish one at Pago Pago, Samoa. In the early 1860s a temporary coaling station had been established in Hawaii, but was abandoned a short time later. At that time, the Navy still leaned heavily towards sail power and had little use for permanent coaling stations. In 1884, after a series of negotiations with King Kalakaua of Hawaii, the United States was granted exclusive rights to enter Pearl Harbor and establish a coaling and repair station.

The second type of facility developed after the Civil War was the Naval Torpedo Station at Newport, Rhode Island. The Navy established the station in 1869 as an experimental station for the development of torpedoes and torpedo equipment, explosives, and electrical equipment. Situated on Goat Island, the station served primarily as a school for the instruction of naval officers on the manufacture and use of torpedoes. An old frame house was converted into a temporary machine shop, and a magazine and laboratory were constructed soon after the facility was established.

With the acquisition of Alaska in 1867 and the expansion of American shipping in the Pacific, the need for docking and repair facilities north of Mare Island, California, became readily evident. In 1888, Congress authorized the Navy to construct a yard north of the forty-second parallel in either the State of Oregon or the Territory of Washington. The Navy assigned Lt. Ambrose B. Wyckoff to select and purchase land for establishing a Navy facility. Lt. Wyckoff acquired 191 acres at Port Orchard, on Puget Sound, for $10,000 and, in 1891, became the first commandant of the new naval station. One year later a contract for a state-of-the-art stone dry dock 650 feet in length, 130 feet in width, and 39 feet deep was awarded to Byron Barlow and Company of Tacoma, Washington.

Proper support for development and maintenance of the shore establishment did not last long after the Civil War ended. During the 1880s, Secretary of the Navy William Chandler believed the Navy spent too much money on sustaining and staffing the navy yards and facilities. As a result, in 1883 he closed the Pensacola, Philadelphia, and New London yards, discontinued the construction and repair of ships in Boston, and reduced the size of the Portsmouth yard. This policy remained in effect until the Spanish-American War, and was one of the main factors why the Navy was ill prepared for the conflict.

In 1897, the Bunce Board revealed the inadequacies of the Navy's dry docks and proposed a program to expand and repair them. The board recommended constructing six large graving docks and three steel floating dry docks in order to raise naval station capabilities to the minimum requirements necessary should a conflict arise. The Navy ignored the recommendations until after the Spanish-American War began. The war with Spain had severely taxed the Navy's shore facilities in 1898, but particularly hard hit were the Key West Naval Station and the coaling station in Dry Tortugas, Florida, due to their proximity to Cuba. The New York, Norfolk, and Mare Island facilities, best fitted for the immediate ship repair and maintenance necessary during the brief conflict, were stretched beyond their limits because the other yards were not in any condition to handle extensive work.

The Navy finally recognized its facility deficiencies and ultimately took steps to provide modern shops, improve waterfronts, build superior dry docks, and construct advanced coaling facilities. Congress first authorized the construction of four timber graving docks to be built at Portsmouth, Boston, Philadelphia, and Mare Island on May 4, 1898.

The period from the Spanish-American War to the beginning of World War I was one of extensive growth for the shore establishment. The Portsmouth and Boston yards, which had been practically closed for many years, began constructing various shops and buildings, and installing modern machinery for the repair of ships' hulls and engines. The Navy expanded facilities at other yards, especially Norfolk and Philadelphia. By 1901, the yards and stations, which previously lacked the basics to maintain the fleet, had modernized services enough to meet Navy standards, allowing the building, repair, and maintenance of ships to increase. The bases entered a never before seen period of activity and transformation.

One of the major naval construction projects that grew out of the Spanish-American War was the Panama Canal project. Shortly after the USS *Maine* exploded, the Navy ordered the USS *Oregon* from San Francisco, California, to Key West, Florida, to join the fleet before continuing on to Santiago, Cuba. However, before it could join the fleet it had to journey 16,000 miles around South America and the tip of Cape Horn to reach its destination. The journey took 69 days to complete, which convinced the American government that it was a matter of national security to create a shorter route between the Atlantic and Pacific Oceans.

The U.S. had contemplated the Isthmian Canal early in 1874, when President Grant sent an expedition to Central America to survey a possible canal route. The U.S. began a canal route through Nicaragua, including eleven miles of railroad and two miles of excavation; however, the financial panic of 1891 halted the project.

President McKinley refocused attention on the Isthmus of Panama, and formed the Isthmus Canal Commission in 1899 to study the possibility of completing the Panama Canal project, which had been abandoned by French engineers. The Army Corps of Engineers, headed by Lieutenant Colonel George W. Goethals and assisted by Civil Engineer Corps Officer Rear Admiral Harry Rousseau, completed the partially excavated canal. Rousseau was responsible for all construction of canal related structures, all municipal engineering, and the motor power requirements. Under the direction of Rousseau ten thousand employees built the locks, cranes, and fueling depots. He designed and oversaw construction of the Atlantic and Pacific terminals of the canal, including the harbors, docks, piers, coaling plants, quay walls, dry dock, and repair shops.

In accordance with the Panamanian treaty ratified by Congress in 1904, the Navy established several stations within the Canal Zone. In order to maintain contact with Radio Arlington and San Diego, California, the Navy established a high-powered Naval Radio Station at Darien, Panama Canal Zone, in 1914. The station was equipped with a powerhouse, operator's building, quarters, and storehouses. In 1917, the Navy established two bases in the Canal Zone: Coco Solo, on the Caribbean side, and Balboa on the Pacific Coast. Both stations maintained secondary radio equipment, coal, fuel oil, and lighterage facilities.

View looking north from the walk leading toward the dry dock, Puget Sound Naval Station, Bremerton, Washington, c. 1896-1897. Structures seen in the distance include (from left-center to right): the flagstaff and hospital (former office building); pumping house; and wharf. In the middle distance are the pontoon bridge, with a whaleboat under repair on its deck and the small yard tug *Fucca* alongside. At the bridge end is the barracks ship *Nipsic*. Partially visible beyond *Nipsic* is the U.S. Coast Guard Ship *Hassler*. *Courtesy of the Naval History and Heritage Command, Collection of Rear Admiral Ammen C. Farenholt, USN(MC).*

Photograph taken at the Mare Island Navy Yard from Radio Hill, southwest of the naval hospital looking northwest about 1872. The old marine barracks are visible to the left and the sectional dry dock is visible to the right. Mare Island grew rapidly at this time, with the construction of a wharf, shops, sheds, and houses for the officers. The grounds were leveled and the streets paved. A sectional dock was assembled and the basin and marine railway were completed, making the navy yard functional. *Courtesy of the U.S. Navy Seabee Museum.*

General view of the Mare Island Navy Yard taken from Radio Hill looking northwest, January 12, 1940 (same view as image on the left). The borrow pit is visible on the left side of the hill on middle ground, and the Old Marine barracks are still visible on the left. *Courtesy of the U.S. Navy Seabee Museum.*

In 1900 the Navy, fearing attack by Spanish warships, established a General Board to insure efficient preparation of the fleet in case of war and for the naval defense of the coast. In 1902, Secretary John Davis Long reported to Congress that better results could be attained in properly defending the U.S. coast by developing and organizing the naval defense into a system of districts. The Navy divided the coast into three sections to experiment with the new system. Based on the experiment, the General Board devised a more comprehensive plan. This recommendation led to the formal establishment of the naval district system on May 7, 1903. Naval leadership created thirteen naval districts modeled directly after the existing lighthouse district system. This new system, which included the continental U.S., all island possessions, and the Canal Zone, managed the administration and operations of the shore establishment. A commandant, usually a rear admiral, who in general directed all naval activities in his district, headed each district. Commandants also operated all patrol and other craft in their districts, prepared and executed war plans for their districts, and cooperated with the Army in coastal defense. In 1916, the Navy extended the naval district system to include Puerto Rico and Hawaii, two of the outlying possessions. At this time, the Navy also added a distinct staff and began to separate the district offices from other commands. By 1920, the naval district boundaries were no longer restricted to confined strips of seacoast, but enlarged to include whole groups of states, with the entire United States and most of the outlying possessions divided among them.

By the early twentieth century, the Navy decided to invest in the new technology of aircraft. After the successful flights of the Wright brothers, as well as other early pioneer pilots, the Navy began exploring the idea of aircraft. Pilot Eugene Ely first demonstrated the possibility of teaming airplanes and ships when he flew his Curtiss biplane off the altered deck of the cruiser USS *Birmingham* in November 1910. Two months later, on January 18, 1911, Ely landed his airplane on a platform built on the armored cruiser USS *Pennsylvania* anchored in San Francisco Bay, using the first ever tail hook system. These demonstrations convinced Navy leaders that the airplane had a future with the Navy.

Naval aviation began on a small newly constructed airfield at Greenbury Point, Maryland, in 1911. The new aviation groups abandoned the cleared space a short time later since the land was too small for planes, too close to the Naval Academy's rifle range, and the water too shallow for hydroplanes. During the winter of 1913, the Navy chose Guantanamo Bay, Cuba, as the second aviation training base. Shortly thereafter the Navy decided a main aeronautics station was needed, and in January 1914 the facility in Pensacola was re-designated the first Naval Aeronautic Station. The first naval aviation unit assigned to Pensacola consisted of nine officers, less than two dozen enlisted men, and had only eleven airplanes.

Since the beginning of the Spanish-American War naval public works had expanded, but its growth was not proportionate with the fleet. A thorough survey of naval resources was made in 1914, shortly after the beginning of World War I, and it became evident that if the country were drawn into war numerous additions to the fleet, the naval shore facilities, and the merchant marine would be required.

In 1916, prior to joining World War I, the United States started a gigantic six-year program of naval expansion. In that year Congress allowed the Navy to contract for 813,000 tons of new vessels, the biggest step toward naval power the U.S. had taken thus far in its history. From 1916 to 1922 the Navy added 10 battleships, 1 aircraft carrier, 287 destroyers, and 88 submarines to the fleet. This process, which would place the United States second on the list of world naval powers, taxed the naval shipbuilding facilities and exceeded their capabilities early on.

The U.S. completed an enormous amount of construction during the first six months of its involvement in World War I, including building training facilities, hospital facilities, shipyard development, dry docks, power plants, ordnance depots, and storage facilities. The Shore Station Development Board, established in 1916, served the dual purpose of coordinating the various Bureau public works programs and making general long-range plans to guide the development of the shore establishment.

The Navy underwent phenomenal growth in materiel and personnel during 1917 and 1918. Until the United States entered the war, naval public works were confined to the continental states and its territories. During the war, the United States constructed a multitude of public works services in France and Great Britain to support the fleet and aid its allies in the tenuous years afterward.

The total expenditures for all public works carried out under the supervision of the Bureau of Yards and Docks from 1916-1918 were more than the total expenditure that had been made at all navy yards and naval stations during the preceding 116 years. The overall naval public works more than doubled in value from about $211 million to $469 million.

Many of the postwar problems confronting the Bureau of Yards and Docks in 1919 and 1920 included the salvage and disposition of surplus materials, berthing for deactivated ships, and deactivation or disposal of disestablished stations, hospitals, and training camps. The Navy salvaged and transferred property and equipment to other activities, including the Veteran's Bureau. The government sold anything that could not be used to its advantage under competitive bids to the highest bidder.

Photograph of the Navy Department and Munitions Building under construction, facing towards the Washington Memorial, 1918. Contractors built and used the temporary structures on the far right as a commissary, storerooms, and barracks for the men. The buildings were located where the Reflecting Pool now lies between the Washington and Lincoln memorials. *Courtesy of the U.S. Navy Seabee Museum.*

Torpedo shop at the Washington Navy Yard, 1917. At the beginning of World War I, the Naval Gun Factory was working at maximum capacity in order to supply the largest proportion of ordnance for the Navy. Shortly after the outbreak of war, plans were made and work began on an immense gun shop capable of assembling and machining naval guns of the highest caliber. Contractors also began construction of a brass foundry; a steel foundry; a forge shop; a pattern shop; an optical shop with its range-finder testing tower; and a five-story machine shop. Prior to the war, the Bureau of Ordnance developed the design and details for high caliber torpedoes so that, if war broke out, plans were on hand to manufacture large numbers of torpedoes. These plans included the provision of additional assembly, overhaul, and storage facilities. *Courtesy of the Library of Congress.*

At the outbreak of war the Navy initiated airship development in this country, and research continued after the armistice. The Navy built its first lighter-than-air station with a massive dirigible hangar at Lakehurst, New Jersey, in 1921. Naval Air Station Lakehurst underwent an enormous construction program in the early 1920s that included the building of Hangar 1, an unprecedented structure at 258 feet wide and 800 feet long with a maximum clear height of 172 feet. The hangar sufficiently housed the dirigibles *Los Angeles* and *Akron,* as well as several smaller airships simultaneously.

The Navy's shore facilities diminished after the Harding administration introduced extreme economic measures throughout the federal government that included a policy of military reduction. Some of the areas that continued to thrive despite curtailments were the Naval Experimental and Research Laboratory in Washington, District of Columbia, and new docking facilities built in Boston, Massachusetts; Kittery, Maine; Norfolk, Virginia; Charleston, South Carolina; Pearl Harbor, Territory of Hawaii; Hunter's Point, California; and Puget Sound, Washington. Most facilities received new sources of power and fire suppression systems in the 1920s. During the 1930s, the Navy modernized lighting systems and equipped many of its facilities with telephone systems and elevators.

During the early thirties, the Defense Establishment operated at an extremely low level of efficiency. However, the Great Depression and the increasing threat from Germany in the latter part of the 1930s greatly affected the Bureau of Yards and Docks and its work. Under the first Deficiency Act of 1931, the Bureau began a construction program of public works which not only provided a new and much-needed field of employment, but also gave the shore establishment vital improvements. The Bureau also administered all funds allotted to the Navy under the Works Progress Administration.

In response to the growing unrest in Europe during the late 1930s, the United States began developing military equipment, work force, and infrastructure plans to prepare for the Axis threat. The Vinson Act authorized the first significant naval expansion after World War I in May 1938, which called for a 20 percent increase in ships and an increase in aircraft strength to 3,000 planes. The law also directed the Secretary of the Navy to appoint a board to determine what additional shore facilities would be needed to support the newly enlarged fleet.

On June 7, 1938, acting Secretary of the Navy Charles Edison appointed the Hepburn Board to make an exhaustive survey of the Navy's strategic defense needs and report all facility deficiencies. In a December 1938 report to Congress, the Hepburn Board stated that the greatest current need was for air bases. The board recommended the establishment of new naval air stations and the expansion of existing air facilities to provide three major air bases on each coast, one in the Canal Zone, and one in the Territory of Hawaii, with outlying operating bases in the West Indies, Alaska, and at each of the U.S. possessions in the Pacific.

Once approved and funded by Congress, the Bureau of Yards and Docks approved two huge construction contracts in 1939: one for bases in the Atlantic and one for those in the Pacific. This major shore expansion program began with the development of air bases at Midway Island; Johnston Island; Palmyra Atoll; Kaneohe Bay, Territory of Hawaii; Kodiak and Sitka, Alaska; San Juan, Puerto Rico; Jacksonville, Florida; Alameda, California; and Quonset Point, Rhode Island. The Bureau also expedited the signing of contracts for new and enlarged naval bases within the continental United States to help prepare the country for war. Nonetheless, when war broke out in Europe in September 1939, the naval shore establishment was woefully unprepared for the global war ahead.

The Bureau of Yards and Docks, with advance base construction the main focus, began developing plans to meet the various technical problems it might face in case of war. In the summer of 1939, studies commenced to develop mobile and standardized equipment which allowed advanced preparation and rapid base construction. Most of the equipment necessary was not commercially available, which required the Bureau to work out basic designs and specifications for mass production. Several of these items included floating dry docks, pontoons, portable housing, portable power plants, and water distillation plants. The Bureau also standardized plans for barracks, warehouses, aircraft hangars, and ammunition magazines of various sizes in order to facilitate rapid base expansion.

View of the Arlington Memorial Bridge and the Navy Department and Munitions Building shortly after the completion of the Lincoln Memorial and Reflecting Pool, c. 1927. Located on the National Mall, the reflecting pool is approximately 2,029 feet long and 167 feet wide. It was designed by Henry Bacon and constructed in 1922 and 1923, following the dedication of the Lincoln Memorial. *Courtesy of the U.S. Navy Seabee Museum.*

Bridge over the Pago Pago River, Guam, built in 1918 by the Navy's Public Works Department, c. 1924. At this time, the Civil Engineer Corps was charged with administering and maintaining the civil public works as well as the naval public works on Guam, the Virgin Islands, and Samoa. *Courtesy of the U.S. Navy Seabee Museum.*

The Two-Ocean Navy Act, approved on July 19, 1940, outlined a formidable shipbuilding program to create two separate but balanced fleets in the Pacific and Atlantic Oceans. The $4 billion program to build 257 additional ships would take eight years to complete, and would increase the total fleet tonnage by 70 percent. The bases built as part of the Hepburn Board were not enough to support the future expansion of the fleet, nor for the daunting conflict ahead. As a result, the Two-Ocean Navy Act also authorized an expenditure of $150 million for essential equipment and facilities to build or equip naval vessels; $65 million for the manufacture of ordnance material and

The submarines USS *Montauk* (left) and USS *Lehigh* laid up at the Philadelphia Navy Yard, Pennsylvania, c. late 1902 or early 1903. A principal ironclad in the naval attack on Charleston, the *Montauk* departed the New York Navy Yard on December 24, 1862, to join the South Atlantic Blockading Squadron. Both monitors were decommissioned and sold in 1904. *Courtesy of the Naval History and Heritage Command.*

munitions; and $35 million for the expansion of armament production facilities. During the period 1938-1945, the Bureau of Yards and Docks awarded 7,427 construction contracts totaling more than $8.7 billion to expand existing facilities and establish new installations.

In 1940, the bases under construction as part of the Hepburn Report were still in the early stages, and the Navy had no properly equipped advance base except Pearl Harbor, which had recently become the central base for the Pacific Fleet. In November 1940, naval construction work increased when the United States agreed to transfer fifty destroyers to the British in exchange for numerous 99-year leases that allowed the U.S. to build naval bases at Argentia, Bermuda, Trinidad, St. Lucia, Jamaica, Great Exuma Island, and British Guiana. Contract work immediately began with civilian labor.

From 1940-1941, the Bureau of Yards and Docks assessed the issue of contractors working in possible hazardous areas and devised a plan. In October 1941, the Bureau of Yards and Docks organized four

USS *D-3* (left) and USS *D-2* (center) at the Philadelphia Navy Yard, Pennsylvania, March 5, 1919, with shipyard workmen on board. A derrick barge is alongside *D-2*. During World War I, D-2 served in training and experimental work at the New London Submarine Base. The Navy placed her in reserve status at the Philadelphia Navy Yard on September 9, 1919 and, finally, decommissioned and sold her hulk for scrap in 1922. *Courtesy of the Naval History and Heritage Command.*

100-man military units called Headquarters Construction Companies to act as administrative units at advance bases in case war broke out during construction. This original company became the nucleus for the First Naval Construction Detachment and was the beginning of the Naval Construction Force.

After war began, the Bureau of Yards and Docks could no longer utilize service contractors and their civilian employees in combat zones. Under military law, contractors and their civilian labor force could not offer resistance when under attack. Any civilian bearing arms would be considered a guerilla, and would be liable to summary execution if captured. Civilian labor also lacked the military training to defend themselves or the facility. This hard lesson was learned when the naval bases at Wake, Cavite, and Guam were overtaken by the Japanese on December 7-8, 1941, and the surviving men, whether military or civilian, were either executed or taken prisoner.

The Bureau of Yards and Docks argued that only military personnel under direct military leadership could complete construction work on advance bases in combat zones and, in response, created the Naval Construction Battalions, better known as the Seabees, to build the Navy's advance bases around the world. Their accomplishments during

Photograph of the Commandant's House at the New York Navy Yard, April 4, 1905. The Navy first defined the duties of the Commandant of the Yard in the 1818 Navy Regulations, placing them under the direction of the Secretary of the Navy. The Commandant employed control over every department in the yard and was responsible for the maintenance and protection of all buildings, stores, vessels, and for prudent appointment and all labor. *Courtesy of the U.S. Navy Seabee Museum.*

Public Works clerical staff at the Puget Sound Naval Shipyard, c. 1936. On January 28, 1911, the House Naval Affairs Committee charged the Bureau of Yards and Docks with the design and construction of the public works and public utilities of the Navy, irrespective of the Bureau or office of the Navy Department that used or operated them. Prior to this time, each Bureau constructed buildings and utilities, and purchased assets independently without care for their fellow naval neighbors and without a specific master plan laid out for the base. This new consolidation greatly streamlined expenses and organized the Navy's real property assets. *Courtesy of the U.S. Navy Seabee Museum.*

the war are legendary, including building over 400 advance bases, 111 major airfields, 441 piers, 2,558 ordnance magazines, hospitals to serve 70,000 patients, and housing for 1.5 million men.

The immense accomplishments of the Bureau of Yards and Docks, the Civil Engineer Corps, and the Seabees during World War II, both at home and abroad, were completed with the specific mission to support the fleet through quick action, rapid expansion, and remarkable ingenuity while achieving their objectives. Above all, they had the will and the capacity to support the fleet and accomplish amazing feats during one of the greatest military tribulations in history. These instrumental actions played a key part in globally expanding the naval shore establishment, quickly winning the war, and creating the largest naval power in the world.

Civil Engineer Corps

Although the Civil Engineer Corps (CEC) was not created until 1867, civil engineers have been associated with the public works of the Navy since the beginning of the nineteenth century. In 1801 President Jefferson, after having recommended and obtained the approval of Congress to reduce the size of the Navy, made arrangements to employ Benjamin Henry Latrobe to plan a dry dock in which twelve 44-gun frigates could be mothballed. Although this project never came to fruition, President Jefferson hired Latrobe in 1804 to become the chief engineer of the United States Navy. In 1805, he was engaged to design and plan the Washington Navy Yard.

Congress, impressed with Latrobe's plans for the Washington Navy Yard, ordered President Jefferson to complete a study and examination of all navy yards and prepare master plans for their development and improvement. After Mr. Latrobe died in 1820, the Secretary of the Navy, Smith Thompson, appointed Colonel Loammi Baldwin to assist the Board of Navy Commissioners in conducting the study, which was finally completed in 1829.

The first Navy Civil Engineer Corps officers: B.F. Chandler, F.C. Prindle, W.P.S. Sanger, F.A. Hastings, and Charles Hastings, c. 1860s. The Navy created the Civil Engineer Corps on March 2, 1867. The original duties of the Civil Engineer Corps included the charge, erection, and repair of all buildings, docks, and wharves; supervising the architect; and directing all masters and other workers involved in building public works. Civil Engineer Corps officers were not required to wear a navy uniform until 1881, when the leaf insignia was created. *Courtesy of the U.S. Navy Seabee Museum.*

Officer's Mess Night, or "Dining-in" at the Army-Navy Club, Washington, D.C., December 4, 1913. The dinner was in honor of Commander Alan Parsons, CEC, USN, upon his detachment as Assistant Chief of the Bureau of Yards and Docks. Next, he assumed the duties as Public Works Officer at the Philadelphia Navy Yard. *Courtesy of the U.S. Navy Seabee Museum.*

Simultaneously, in 1827 Loammi Baldwin accepted an appointment from the United States government to design and supervise the graving docks at the Boston and Norfolk shipyards. Due to the distance between the two yards, Latrobe hired civil engineers to represent him at each site. These engineers received the title "Resident Engineers."

By 1832, the Navy Department had become established enough to employ a civil engineer to take charge of the dry docks at all navy yards. From 1826 to 1835, Baldwin made surveys of New York Harbor to determine the best location for a dry dock. However, the work was not carried out until after his death in 1838. When William P.S. Sanger, Resident Engineer in charge of construction of the Norfolk dry dock, completed his assignment in 1836, the Board of Navy Commissioners appointed him Civil Engineer for the Navy Department and added him to their staff.

By 1852, the Secretary of the Navy had appointed several civil engineers under Sanger's direction for duty at the navy yards. The need for uniform handling of construction and maintenance work at these yards prompted Sanger in 1858 to prepare a series of rules. These rules provided regulation and guidance for civil engineers and defined their duties.

From the beginning of Sanger's career with the Navy, he had advocated the establishment of a staff corps of commissioned civil engineers. Before 1867, the navy yards employed civilian employees as civil engineers. Congress passed a law on March 2, 1867, providing that the President might appoint civil engineers confirmed by the Senate. In January 1869, civil engineers appeared for the first time in the Navy Register, a publication of naval officers. In 1871, Congress asserted that civil engineers be given a rank fixed by the President and limited to 10 persons.

Soon after appointment, Civil Engineer of the Navy Sanger wrote a manual outlining the responsibilities of the newly created Civil Engineer Corps (CEC). He stressed that CEC officers employed at a Navy yard needed to function under the direction of the yard commandant and the Chief of the Bureau of Yards and Docks. The engineer had charge of the erection and repair of all buildings, docks, and wharves; supervised the architect; and directed all masters and other workers involved in building public works. The Civil Engineer also prepared plans, estimated costs, itemized the requisite materials, and scheduled each job.

In February 1881, the President conferred relative rank to Civil Engineer Corps officers and set the Corps staff total at 10 officers: one captain, two commanders, three lieutenant commanders, and four lieutenants. After having had relative rank conferred upon them, the Navy instructed civil engineers to wear the uniform of line officers, omitting the star, with the sleeve lace to be on light blue velvet, shoulder straps border embroidered gold, body light blue cloth, and the letters C.E. in Old English embroidered in silver in the center.

In 1898, after years of pressing their case to the Secretary of the Navy, Mordecai Endicott became the first Civil Engineer Corps officer to be appointed Chief of the Bureau of Yards and Docks. Prior to this time line officers held the position of Chief, although Civil Engineer Corps officers made all the technical engineering decisions with respect to the public works throughout the naval shore establishment.

In March 1899, an act abolished the custom of relative rank and conferred actual naval rank on Civil Engineer Corps officers. Members of the CEC continued to be addressed as "Civil Engineer" and "Assistant Civil Engineer" until a 1918 naval regulation stipulated that every naval officer be addressed by rank.

Subsequent to the Spanish-American War, the increase in the amount of public works done under the Bureau of Yards and Docks necessitated increasing the number of officers to twenty-one. An urgent need for more engineers to handle the work under the Bureau became marked each year. The amount of construction work quadrupled after the start of the war, and was scattered over such a vast extent that it was impossible to meet construction deadlines. The number increased in 1903 to twenty-eight civil engineers and 12 assistant civil engineers.

In 1905, the Civil Engineer Corps insignia changed from the Old English letters C.E., worn on the epaulets, shoulder straps, and collar of the service coat to two crossed silver sprigs, each composed of two live oak leaves and an acorn. While the pattern of the corps device remained the same, uniform regulations issued in 1919 specified that it was to be embroidered in gold instead of silver and worn on the sleeve of frock, evening dress, and blue service coats, above the gold lace strips, and on shoulder marks for white service coat and overcoat. By these same regulations, the light blue cloth worn under the sleeve strips, and worn on the shoulder marks since 1899, was abolished as a distinction of the corps.

Vacancies in the grade of assistant civil engineer were appointed from the civilian world until 1906, when appointments were chosen from Naval Academy graduates. In 1913, appointments to the Corps were selected from Ensigns with a minimum of 18 months of sea service. The men were given a 4-month review course at the Naval Academy Post Graduate School, followed by a 2-year course at the Rensselaer Polytechnic Institute at Troy, New York. Upon satisfactory completion of the course, they received a civil engineer degree and a naval commission as assistant civil engineers.

By modern standards, careers in the Civil Engineer Corps were long before World War II. After May 1908, naval officers were eligible to retire after 30 years of honorable service. The majority of CEC officers remained on active duty until they reached retirement age, which was 62 before 1916 and 64 thereafter. CEC officers tended to retire on disability, rather than retire voluntarily after 30 years, and a significant number died of natural causes before they reached retirement.

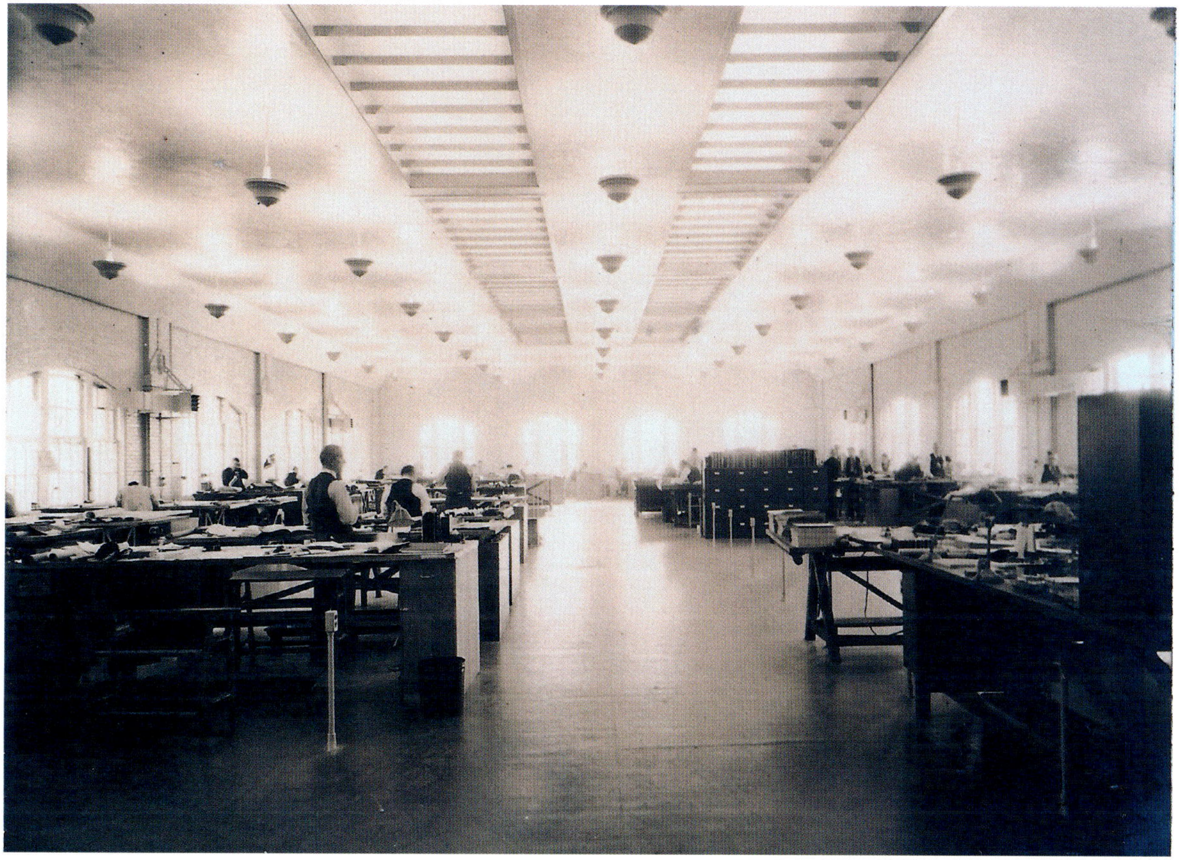

View of the Hull drafting room at the Puget Sound Naval Shipyard, 1936. Designing new buildings and facilities at navy bases remained the responsibility of the Bureau of Yards and Docks in Washington. However, because the officers in the field were familiar with the purpose and need for each structure, as well as the local conditions that might affect construction, close liaison was maintained between the Bureau and the field during the design process. Field participation varied from minor comments to the actual preparation of plans and specifications. Puget Sound Naval Shipyard was one of the few large field commands that handled all of their own design work in house. *Courtesy of the U.S. Navy Seabee Museum.*

Civil Engineer Corps logo after Navy Regulations changed the color from silver to gold, c. 1919. In 1905, the Civil Engineer Corps adopted two crossed silver sprigs, each composed of two live oak leaves and an acorn as their insignia in lieu of the original Old English letters "C.E." In 1919, uniform regulations specified that the insignia be gold instead of silver. *Courtesy of the U.S. Navy Seabee Museum.*

In the early years, the Navy fixed the number of officers at each rank, with most positions in the lower ranks. In this situation, a young officer usually could not hope for a promotion until someone in a higher rank retired or died. The Equalization Act of 1926 attempted to remedy the problem by assigning each staff corps officer a line officer as his "running mate," and making the staff corps officer eligible for promotion at the same time as his running mate. Budgetary constraints continued to limit promotional opportunities for corps officers, and 50-year-old lieutenant commanders were not unusual. Between 1930 and 1940, three career CEC officers retired for age as lieutenant commanders.

Congress passed the Naval Act of August 1916, calling for improvements in the status of CEC officers and establishing the permanent rank of rear admiral. Since 1898, the Chief of the Bureau of Yards and Docks had maintained a temporary rank of rear admiral, held only while he served as Chief. He then reverted to his previous rank for the remainder of his naval career. The act increased the size of the Civil Engineer Corps by setting its strength at 2 percent of the size of the line. Within 2 years, the number of active CEC officers had grown from 41 to more than 75. It also established a Civil Engineer Corps Reserve Force, and during 1917 and 1918 the Navy recruited more than 100 Reserve officers from civilian life.

During the decade prior to World War I, most Civil Engineer Corps officers had served in public works departments at various naval bases, with at least four or five officers in addition to the Chief assigned to the Bureau of Yards and Docks headquarters in Washington. In the 1920s, CEC officers also acquired an important new role as district public works officers. The district public works officer had general cognizance over all public works functions in his naval district, and was the principal representative of the Bureau of Yards and Docks there, as well as the commandant's advisor on public works issues.

The Navy also assigned Civil Engineer Corps officers to detached duties between the World Wars, including the American occupation of Haiti and Santo Domingo between 1915 and 1934 and construction projects on the newly acquired Virgin Islands. The treaty obligations between the U.S. and Santo Domingo and Haiti included conserving revenues, developing the country, and improving the processes and standards of the islands. The Civil Engineer Corps carried out the treaty obligations, which included taking charge of public works and training local engineers. The senior Civil Engineer Corps officer stationed in Haiti was commissioned Engineer-in-Chief to the Haitian government. He headed the Department of Public Works to aid the Haitian Government in the proper and efficient development of its agricultural, mineral, and commercial resources, and to help establish a firm and solid financial base.

In the early thirties, the naval shore establishment operated at an extremely low level of efficiency. Under the first Deficiency Act of 1931 and the Works Program Administration (WPA), the Bureau began a public works construction program, which not only provided employment, but also gave the shore establishment necessary maintenance improvements and began new construction projects. By 1939, the Bureau of Yards and Docks and the Civil Engineer Corps had administered funds allotted to the Navy Department as part of the WPA totaling over $109 million to improve the shore establishment and relieve civilian unemployment.

Heading into World War II, the Civil Engineer Corps comprised only 159 officers, compared with 11,964 at the end of 1945. One of the main reasons for the large number of CEC during World War II was due to the significant portion of wartime construction being conducted under combat conditions at advance bases. The Civil Engineer Corps continues to administer the planning, design, construction, and maintenance of the naval shore establishment, which has grown from the handful of navy yards to a complex group of commands that exist to support the mission of the fleet around the world.

View of the USS *Nebraska* in Dry Dock Number 2 at the Boston Navy Yard on July 21, 1913. Commissioned in 1907, the USS *Nebraska* accompanied the "Great White Fleet" on the remainder of its world cruise starting in May 1908. The *Nebraska* began active wartime service in April 1917, and later, after peace was restored, began a troop transport assignment to bring the U.S. servicemen home from France. The USS *Nebraska* sold for scrap in November 1923 as part of the Washington Naval Limitations Treaty, also known as the Five-Power Treaty of 1922. *Courtesy of the U.S. Navy Seabee Museum.*

Chapter 2: Dry Docks

Early 1847 photograph of Dry Dock Number 1 under construction at the New York Navy Yard. Photograph from a Daguerreotype loaned by Admiral Eugene H.C. Leutze to the Bureau of Yards and Docks in 1898. Begun in 1841, the Bureau constructed the dry dock of granite laid on flagstone and concrete. Completed in 1851 – ten years after it began – at a cost of over $2 million, it could hold a ship 320 feet long with a 49.5-foot beam and a draft of 21 feet. *Courtesy of the U.S. Navy Seabee Museum.*

A dry dock is a narrow basin or vessel that can be flooded to allow a load to be floated in, then drained to allow that load to come to rest on a dry platform. Dry docks are used for the construction, maintenance, and repair of ships, boats, and other watercraft. The two main types of dry docks are floating and graving. Both expose the entire hull of a vessel for purposes of cleaning or repair of vessels. Prior to the invention of dry docks, sailors were required to heave down their ships to caulk or repair the vessels. The graving dry dock has a narrow basin usually made of earthen berms and concrete, closed by gates or by a caisson, into which a vessel may be floated and the water pumped out, leaving the vessel supported on blocks. The keel blocks, as well as the bilge block, are placed on the floor of the dock in accordance with the docking plan of the ship.

In 1825, the Board of Commissioners was finally able to convince Congress of the need for dry docks for repairing ships, frigates, and small vessels. Secretary Samuel Southard recommended the erection of two dry docks: one at Norfolk and one at Boston. Based on Loammi Baldwin's surveys and estimates, the dry docks at the Boston and Norfolk yards were begun in 1827. Because of the distance between Boston and Norfolk, Baldwin appointed engineers Alexander Parris and William P.S. Sanger, respectively, to represent him at each yard. From 1827 to 1834, Baldwin also surveyed New York Harbor to determine the best location for a dry dock at the Navy yard. A third graving dock, begun at the Brooklyn Navy Yard in 1841, was completed in 1851, and dry docking facilities were soon to be available at all seven yards.

View of Dry Dock Number 2 and its surroundings at the Philadelphia Navy Yard, Pennsylvania, August 15, 1919. Inside the dry dock are the USS *Lake Gedney*, in center, and USS *Minnesotan*, partially visible at right. Both ships were being prepared for decommissioning. In the distance is the Reserve Basin, with several older battleships visible, among them USS *Iowa* (Battleship # 4). *Courtesy of the Naval History and Heritage Command.*

Dry docks at Hunter's Point Naval Shipyard, California, holding sailing schooners and merchant vessels, 1907. The community of Hunters Point developed around two graving docks purchased and built up in the late nineteenth and early twentieth century by the Union Iron Works. The Bethlehem Shipbuilding Company purchased the shipbuilding ways in 1905. In 1916, the dry docks were believed to be the largest in the world. At a length of over 1,000 feet, they were said to be sufficient to accommodate the largest warships and passenger steamers afloat. The Navy used the docks as a midway site between San Diego, California, and Bremerton, Washington. *Courtesy of the U.S. Navy Seabee Museum.*

Photograph of Dry Dock Number 1 at the Charleston Navy Yard, South Carolina, in early 1914. The Bureau completed the dry dock on March 16, 1907, when a crane set the last concrete block in place, but the Navy delayed the commissioning until November 1908, when the power plant necessary to drive the pumping machinery was completed. *Courtesy of the U.S. Navy Seabee Museum.*

Meantime, the yards at Portsmouth, Philadelphia, and Pensacola needed docking facilities. On August 3, 1848, Congress approved the construction of a floating dry dock for each yard. By October 1852, the docks at Portsmouth and Philadelphia were completed and were in operation, the Pensacola dock was nearly completed, and the sectional dock for Mare Island had been shipped to the West Coast.

In docking a vessel on the floating dry docks, the pumps were set in motion by the steam engine on the deck above, a gate closed the discharge opening for that purpose, and the water rose in the chamber above the pumps until it was full to the deck of the dock. It is then allowed to flow into the upper chamber of the dock until its weight, acting as ballast, sinks the dock to the required depth. When the ship is floated into the dock and secured, the water is drawn off by means of valves, causing the dock to rise by its own specific gravity until it touches the bottom of the ship.

As early as 1897, the Bunce Board revealed the inadequacies of the Navy's dry docks, and proposed a program to expand and repair them. The Board recommended six large graving docks and three steel floating dry docks to raise naval station capabilities. The Navy ignored the recommendations until after the war began. During the war with Spain in 1898, the Navy's shore facilities were severely taxed – particularly Key West and the coaling station in Dry Tortugas, Florida. The New York, Norfolk, and Mare Island stations, best fitted for the immediate ship repair and maintenance necessary during the brief

Excavation at the head of Dry Dock Number 2 at the Boston Navy Yard, May 15, 1899. Construction began on a new granite and concrete dry dock in 1899 to create the largest of this kind in the world. Dry Dock Number 2 began operation on August 12, 1905, when the USS *Maryland* docked. *Courtesy of the U.S. Navy Seabee Museum.*

conflict, were strained beyond their limits, since the other yards were not in a condition to handle work of any great extent.

It became apparent that the United States, from a naval point of view, was weak in comparison to the great naval powers of Europe. Japan's naval strength was growing rapidly, and surpassed the U.S. by the turn of the nineteenth century. It became necessary to supplement U.S. naval strength by providing accessible places for repair and docking with fortifications located strategically along both coasts.

The first authorization to begin dry dock construction was given on May 4, 1898, for four timber graving docks to be built at Portsmouth, Boston, Philadelphia, and Mare Island. A new program of dry dock construction was initiated, and the Bureau began a project to modernize shops and make improvements to waterfront and berthing facilities throughout the shore establishment. Soon after the Spanish-American War, Congress authorized the construction of three additional graving docks of granite and concrete to be built at the Charleston, Norfolk, and New York navy yards. The dimensions also needed to be at least 650 feet in length; 95 feet in width; with a depth over sill at mean low water of 30 feet; and the floor of the dock to be 4 feet below sill in order to handle the new, larger ships of the fleet.

Seven "O" type submarines in dry dock at the Charleston Navy Yard, South Carolina, c. 1919. USS *O-10* (Submarine # 71) is in the foreground. The most distant "boats" are *O-1* (Submarine # 62) and *O-3* (Submarine # 64). The "O" class submarines were more robust than the previous "L" Class, with greater power and endurance for ocean patrols. The "O" class diesel engines, which began commissioning into the fleet in 1918, were much faster than previous classes. *Courtesy of the Naval History and Heritage Command.*

Sliding ship's cradle in Dry Dock Number 1, Boston Navy Yard, Massachusetts, June 13, 1921. The ship cradle was a support usually made of wood to hold a ship, submarine, or boat upright in the dry dock to allow the vessel to be built or repaired. *Courtesy of the U.S. Navy Seabee Museum.*

When the United States acquired the Philippines from Spain, it also acquired the base at Cavite as part of the peace treaty. The Navy decided it urgently needed a base with a dry dock in the Philippines to repair American vessels in the Pacific. The Navy decided that a floating dry dock, which could easily be relocated if necessary, would best suit the Cavite facility. The Dewey floating steel dry dock – built by the Maryland Steel Company – was designed, constructed, and towed to the naval station. The self-docking, floating steel structure composed of sidewalls and pontoons could expand to five hundred feet in length, had a width of one hundred feet, and could raise a vessel of 16,000 gross tons. The dry dock was towed to the Cavite Naval Station by way of the Mediterranean Sea and the Suez Canal, a distance of 13,000 miles.

By 1916, the Navy had 21 dry docks of all descriptions, including the Balboa dock in the Panama Canal, which had been completed that year. Aside from the Balboa dock, the naval shore establishment at this time could boast only one dock, a 1,002-foot dry dock in Pearl Harbor better than 800 feet in length. At this time two were 740 feet long, and the remaining 18 ranged from 740 feet down to 324 feet, in the case of the Norfolk dry dock.

During the 1920s, the Bureau completed construction and renovation on a series of dry docks over 1,000 feet in length at various naval stations on the Atlantic and Pacific coasts. These docks were fully equipped with all necessary facilities, including air, water, steam, electric power connection, cranes, and capstans. The docks were each equipped with three or four electronically driven pumps, which handled approximately 100,000 gallons of water per minute. Caisson gates with electronically operated pumping equipment were used to remove the water after the ship was placed inside. Although the Navy had improved and expanded its dry dock facilities, it was still woefully unprepared to properly repair and renovate the fleet during the global war ahead.

Interior view of the main deck for the Dry Dock Number 2 caisson, Puget Sound Naval Shipyard, Washington, October 24, 1914. Caisson gates with electronically operated pumping equipment were used to remove the water after the ship was moved into the dry dock. In docking a vessel in a dry dock, the pumps were set in motion by the steam engine on the deck above, and a gate closed the discharge opening. *Courtesy of the U.S. Navy Seabee Museum.*

NAVY YARD NY 7-2
VIEW SHOWING TH
IN DRYDOCK.
CG-6
CG-15

The USS *Utah*, the first vessel docked in Dry Dock Number 4 at the New York Navy Yard, shortly after construction completed, May 9, 1912. Dry Dock Number 4 was funded by congressional appropriation of $1 million in 1905. Twenty men died and over 400 were injured before the all-concrete dry dock was completed in 1912 at a cost of over $3 million. *Courtesy of the U.S. Navy Seabee Museum.*

Workers repairing the altars on the east side at New York Navy Yard's Dry Dock Number 2, looking northwest from head end, July 31, 1913. Altars are the step in the wall of the dry dock upon which the ship's cradle and structures supported a vessel stand. *Courtesy of the U.S. Navy Seabee Museum.*

Dry Dock Number 2 at the New York Navy Yard, showing the USS *McDougal* and USS *Abel P Upshur*, July 27, 1932. In 1886 construction began on Dry Dock Number 2, which required the work of over 400 men daily for three years to complete. *Courtesy of the U.S. Navy Seabee Museum.*

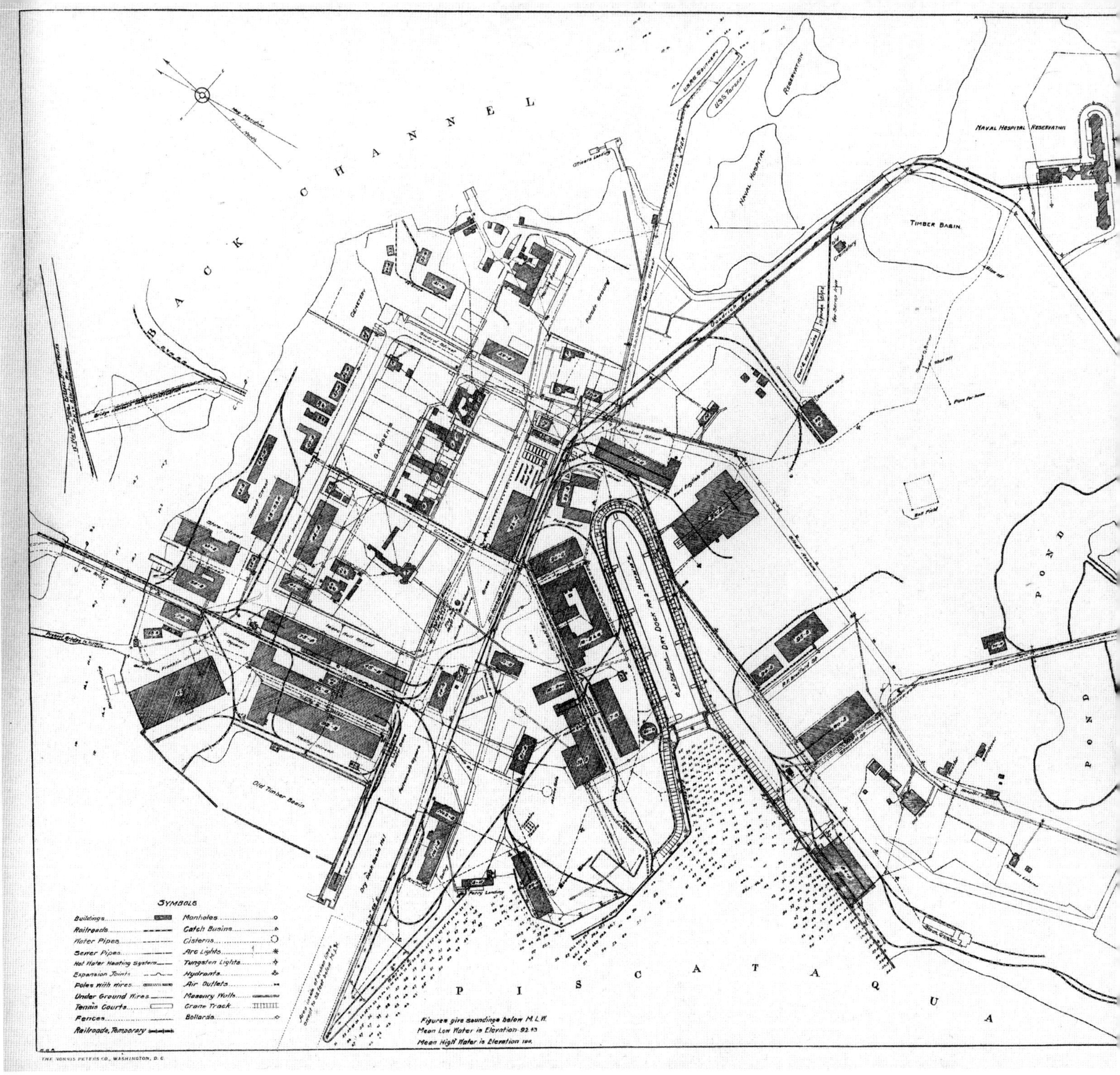

THE NORRIS PETERS CO., WASHINGTON, D. C.

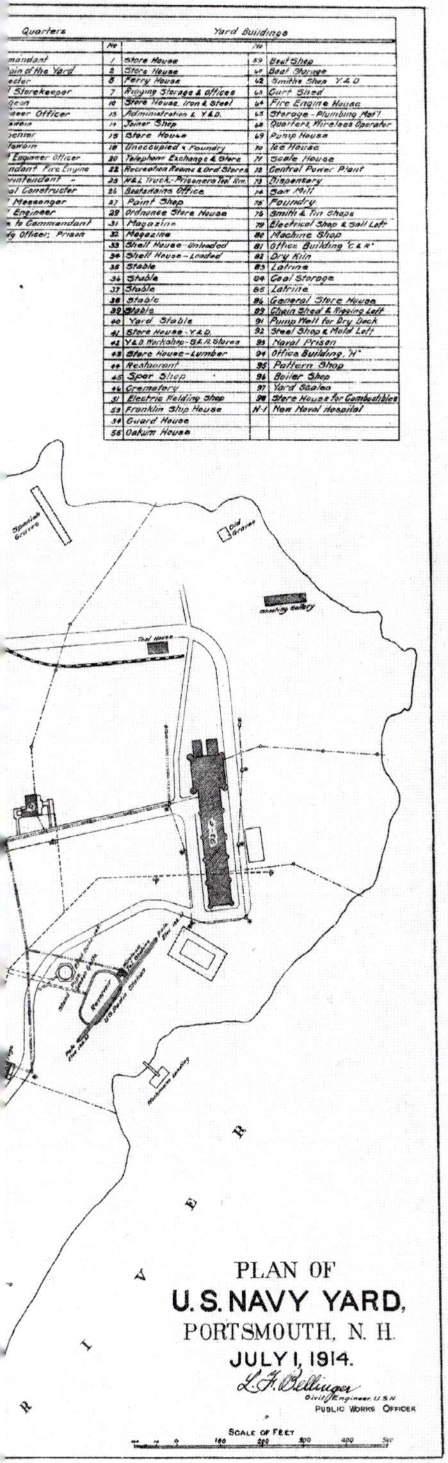

USS *Connecticut* in Dry Dock Number 2 at the Philadelphia Navy Yard, Pennsylvania, August 1913. The dry dock was begun in 1899, but labor and specification problems delayed completion and testing until 1907. In addition, pumping and electrical problems delayed commissioning until 1910. *Courtesy of the U.S. Navy Seabee Museum.*

Plan for the U.S. Navy Yard, Portsmouth, Maine, July 1, 1914. The Portsmouth Naval Shipyard, one of only two of the original six navy yards designed and built by the Navy still in operation, remains an active and resilient part of the Navy's industrial machine. *Courtesy of the U.S. Navy Seabee Museum.*

USS *Montgomery* and USS *Nashville* cradled in Dry Dock Number 2 at the Portsmouth Navy Yard, Maine, looking southwest on August 1, 1913. *Courtesy of the U.S. Navy Seabee Museum.*

Dry Dock Number 2 at the Mare Island Navy Yard, California, looking from the roof of the building southeasterly, June 6, 1935. The Navy installed a one hundred fifty ton revolving crane at the Mare Island Navy Yard specifically for the maintenance of naval ships and submarines. *Courtesy of the U.S. Navy Seabee Museum.*

Caisson for Dry Dock Number 2 at Mare Island Navy Yard, California, ready to launch at the Union Iron Works, San Francisco, April 3, 1908. The contractor then towed the caisson from the Union Iron Works to the Mare Island Navy Yard, floated it into place, and then positioned the caisson into the grooves at the end of Dry Dock Number 2. *Courtesy of the U.S. Navy Seabee Museum.*

Seven "O" type submarines in dry dock at the Charleston Navy Yard, South Carolina, c. 1919. USS *O-1* (Submarine # 62) is in the foreground. USS *O-3* (Submarine # 64) is next astern, to left. USS *O-10* (Submarine # 71) is the most distant, in the right center. The dry dock is in the process of being filled. *Courtesy of the Naval History and Heritage Command.*

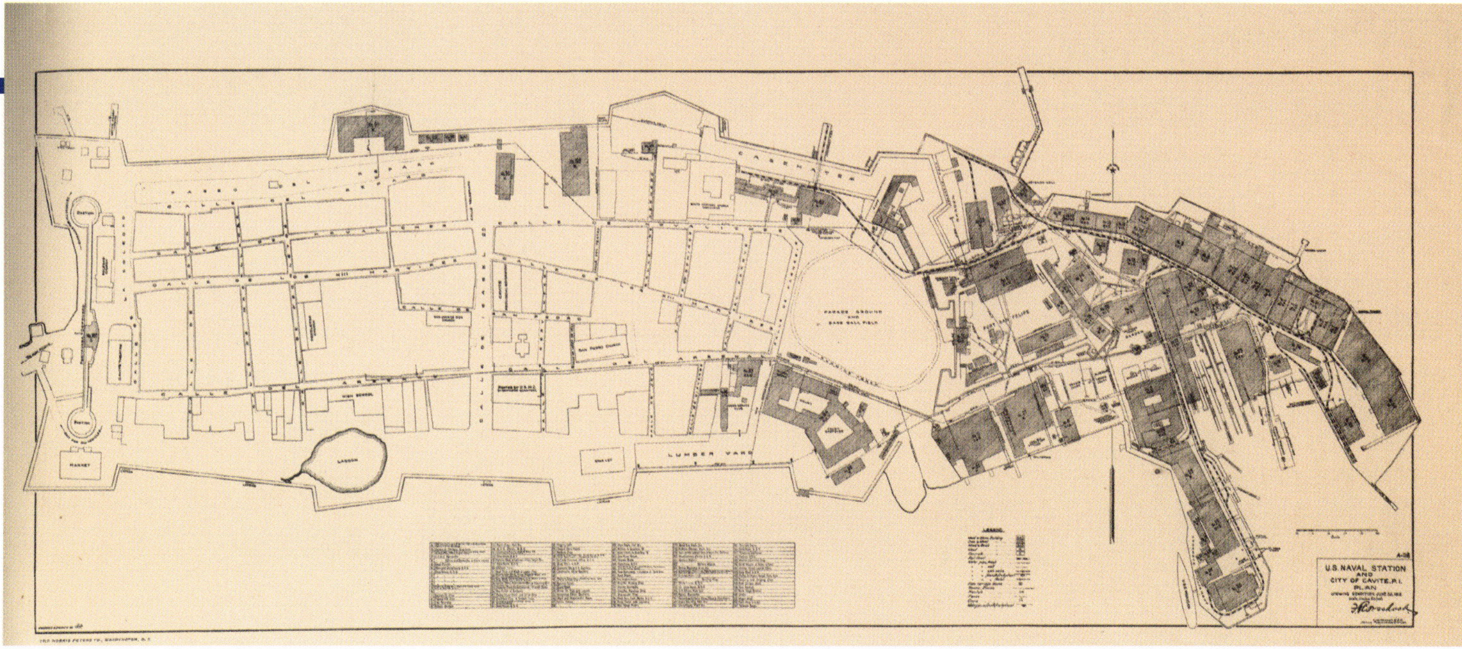

Map of the U.S. Naval Station Cavite, Philippines, 1914, drawn by the Public Works Department. As a result of the Spanish-American War, the 1898 Treaty of Paris allowed temporary American control of Cuba and, following their purchase from Spain, unspecified colonial authority over Puerto Rico, Guam, and the Philippines. In 1902, the first Civil Engineer Corps officer arrived in Cavite to establish the first Public Works office and begin constructing a base infrastructure. *Courtesy of the U.S. Navy Seabee Museum.*

USS *Milwaukee* (Cruiser # 21) in dry dock while receiving an overhaul at the Mare Island Navy Yard, California, April 27, 1916. The Union Iron Works of San Francisco, California, laid down the second *Milwaukee* (C-21) on July 30, 1902, launched her on September 10, 1904, and commissioned her December 10, 1906. *Courtesy of the Naval History and Heritage Command.*

Workers spread concrete and pour the tunnel section for the floor section of Dry Dock Number 3 at the Puget Sound Naval Shipyard, Washington, March 9, 1931. The contractors made the concrete floor to a 20-foot thickness to overcome any hydrostatic buoyancy to which the dry dock might be subjected. *Courtesy of the U.S. Navy Seabee Museum.*

General view of Dry Dock Number 1 construction showing sections in place at the Pearl Harbor Naval Base, Territory of Hawaii, March 8, 1919. Hawaiian Dredging Company completed dredging the basin at the Pearl Harbor Naval Base to construct Dry Dock Number 1. A new method of constructing a dry dock was tried which included dividing the 1,000-foot dock into 16 sections and constructing the shell of each section base on a floating dry dock. *Courtesy of the U.S. Navy Seabee Museum.*

Filling Dry Dock Number 1 through caisson to test pumps at the Pearl Harbor Naval Base after its completion in July 1919. The Pearl Harbor dry dock was designed to provide for a usable length of 1,029 feet, so that it could take any ship which could pass through the Panama Canal. *Courtesy of the U.S. Navy Seabee Museum.*

USS *SP-467* in Dry Dock Number 1 at the Pearl Harbor Naval Base, Territory of Hawaii, c. 1920-21. Commissioned the civilian ship *Delaware*, the *SP-467* also served in the Navy as *AT-53* and *YT-111*. *Courtesy of the Naval History and Heritage Command.*

Destroyers in Dry Dock Number 2 at the Puget Sound Naval Shipyard, Washington, having modified after-deckhouses installed to carry the after 4"/50 guns, September 1922. The destroyers are, from left to right: USS *Moody* (DD-277), USS *Henshaw* (DD-278), and USS *Meyer* (DD-279). *Courtesy of the Naval History and Heritage Command.*

The USS G-1 (Submarine 19½) in dry dock. The 400-ton Lake type submarine was laid down at Newport News, Virginia, in 1909, and commissioned in 1912. Her first years in service were spent operating with the Atlantic Torpedo Flotilla. From the middle of 1915, she was employed in experimental and training duties in the Long Island Sound area. The USS *G-1* was decommissioned in March 1920 and destroyed in depth charge tests in June 1921. *Courtesy of the Naval History and Heritage Command and Donald M. McPherson.*

Yard workers labor on the Hercules crane during routine maintenance at New York Navy Yard dry dock, looking northwest, February 28, 1911. A typical navy yard provided floating derricks and cranes of capacities varying from 15 to 150 tons to assist shore cranes in the fitting out of vessels and repairing of ships. *Courtesy of the U.S. Navy Seabee Museum.*

USS *Kanawha* (Fuel Ship #13) in dry dock at the Philadelphia Navy Yard, Pennsylvania, March 3, 1919. Two submarines are also in dry dock, with USS *L-3* in the foreground. The USS *Kanawha* is still painted in World War I "dazzle" patterned camouflage. *Courtesy of the Naval History and Heritage Command.*

Photograph of USS *L-8* in dry dock at the Portsmouth Navy Yard, Kittery, Maine, 1917. USS *Leonides* is in the left background with a gun installed on her forecastle. The round building in the right center is the dry dock pump house. Following training operations along the east coast, *L-8* prepared for European service to join the fleet during World War I. She steamed for the Azores to join Submarine Division 6 in ASW patrols. *Courtesy of the Naval History and Heritage Command.*

Workers scraping the USS *Northern Pacific's* hull side in preparation for repainting while she is in Dry Dock Number 3 at the New York Navy Yard, February-May 1919. She was undergoing repair for damages received after grounding off Fire Island, New York, on January 1, 1919. *Courtesy of the Naval History and Heritage Command.*

USS *O-1* (Submarine # 62) in dry dock at the Portsmouth Navy Yard, Maine, on September 5, 1918. *O–1*, the first of its class of submarine, was laid down March 26, 1917, at the Portsmouth Navy Yard; launched 9 July 1918; and commissioned at Portsmouth on November 5, 1918. *Courtesy of the Naval History and Heritage Command.*

Photograph of the cofferdam at the Puget Sound Naval Shipyard, Washington, looking southeast, May 4, 1909. A cofferdam is an enclosure within a water environment constructed to allow water to be pumped out to lay bare a portion of a submerged surface and create a dry work environment. The Navy also uses the cofferdam on occasion in the shipbuilding and ship repair industry when it is not practical to put a ship in dry dock for repair or alteration. *Courtesy of the National Archives.*

Setting "A" course in Dry Dock Number 2 at the Puget Sound Naval Shipyard, Washington, on February 8, 1911. Dry Dock Number 2 was made of concrete with sides faced with granite, and was the largest dock built in the United States at the time of completion. The USS *Oregon,* the first ship to successfully dock in Dry Dock Number 2, entered on March 1, 1913. *Courtesy of the National Archives.*

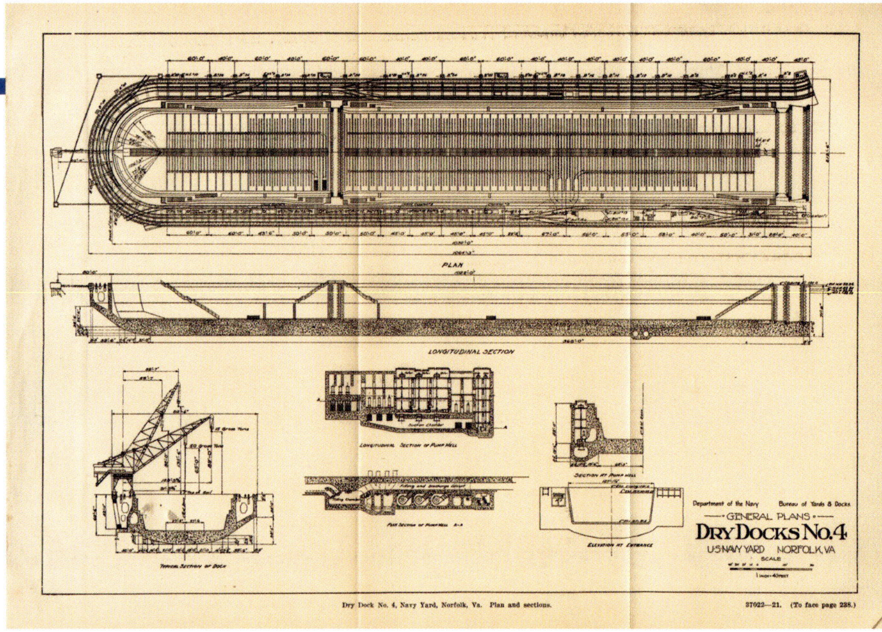

General plans for Dry Dock Number 4 at the Norfolk Navy Yard, Virginia, c. World War I. Begun before the declaration of war, Dry Dock Number 4 measured 1,011 feet from the head of the dock to the side of the caisson. Its width at the coping is 144 feet, with its depth over the keep blocks at 40 feet. *Courtesy of the U.S. Navy Seabee Museum.*

USS *Mahopac* (AT-29), in center, and five destroyers cradled in Dry Dock Number 2 at the Puget Sound Naval Shipyard, Washington, September 1921. The destroyers include USS *Doyen* (DD-280), USS *Henshaw* (DD-278), USS *McCawley* (DD-276), USS *Meyer* (DD-279), and USS *Moody* (DD-277). *Courtesy of Naval History and Heritage Command*

USS *Constitution* enters Dry Dock Number 1 at the Boston Navy Yard, June 16, 1927, with a crowd of over 10,000 observers watching. In 1924, the Naval Board of Surveys and Inspection compiled a report on the condition of the *Constitution* and found her in grave condition. From 1927 to 1930, she spent three years in dry dock undergoing extensive repairs, including installing water piping throughout, modern toilet and shower facilities, and electric lighting to make the interior visible for visitors. She remains in commission today as a museum ship and is the oldest ship on the Navy List. *Courtesy of the U.S. Navy Seabee Museum.*

Civil Engineer Calvin Brown, Officer in Charge of Public Works construction, standing on the stone blocks at Dry Dock Number 1 at the Mare Island Navy Yard, California, on December 1, 1878. Construction of the new dry dock began December 1, 1874, and finished February 18, 1891. Dry Dock Number 1 was Mare Island's only stone dock, while the others were concrete. *Courtesy of the National Archives.*

The USS *Saratoga* comes into Dry Dock Number 2 after an extension was completed at the Puget Sound Naval Shipyard, Washington, November 17, 1930. In order to allow larger ships access, the dry dock was extended to 867 feet. In 1938 plans were drawn to build Dry Dock Number 4, a 1,000-foot dry dock designed to accommodate the existing battleships and the larger, newly planned ships. *Courtesy of the National Archives.*

USS *Milwaukee* in Dry Dock No 2 at the Puget Sound Naval Shipyard, Washington, on June 1, 1913. The second *Milwaukee* (C-21) was laid down July 30, 1902, at Union Iron Works in San Francisco and launched September 10, 1904. After being placed in reserve status in 1908 at the Puget Sound Navy Yard, she was decommissioned May 3, 1910. The *Milwaukee* recommissioned in ordinary June 17, 1913, and was assigned to the Pacific Reserve Fleet. The *Milwaukee* decommissioned March 6, 1917, and in November 1918, was destroyed when a storm broke the ship in two. *Courtesy of the National Archives.*

View looking aft from just forward of the bow of the USS *Von Steuben* while the ship was in dry dock at the New York Navy Yard, February 26, 1919. A recently fitted underwater listening device is visible on both sides, low on the hull just aft of the bow. Also seen are paravane chains running from the deck down to the fitting at the base of the stern. *Courtesy of the Naval History and Heritage Command.*

USS *Pike* (Submarine #6) hauled out on a marine railway at San Diego Naval Station, California, c. 1910. The first *Pike* (SS–6) was commissioned May 28, 1903, but was later renamed *A–5* on November 17, 1911. *Courtesy of the Naval History and Heritage Command, Collection of Donald M. McPherson.*

Dry Dock Number 4 at the Norfolk Navy Yard, Virginia, February 18, 1908, showing the locomotive crane around the dry dock. These early cranes were mounted on railroad tracks to allow easy movement around the dry dock and shipyard. *Courtesy of the Naval History and Heritage Command.*

Submarines *A-6* (Submarine #7), *A-4* (Submarine #5), and *A-2* (Submarine #3) in the Dewey Floating Dry Dock at the Olongapo Naval Station, Philippines, c. 1912. The bow of the tender USS *Mohican* is at the left with an anchor suspended from her starboard cathead. A steam sloop of war, the second USS *Mohican* was laid down at the Mare Island Navy Yard on September 4, 1872. After first being assigned to the Pacific Squadron and later the Bering Sea Squadron and Asiatic Squadron, she served as a station ship in Cavite from 1910 until decommissioned in 1921. *Courtesy of the Naval History and Heritage Command, Collection of Phillip H. Wilson*

Photograph of the USS *S-4* in dry dock after the Navy salvaged it from the bottom of Cape Cod Bay, March 1928. On December 17, 1927, while surfacing from a submerged run over the measured-mile off Provincetown, Cape Cod, Massachusetts, the U.S. Coast Guard vessel *Paulding* accidentally rammed and sunk her. Efforts were made, but were unsuccessful, to rescue six known survivors trapped in the forward torpedo room. The *S-4* was finally raised on March 17, 1928, and towed to the Boston Navy Yard for dry repair. *Courtesy of the Naval History and Heritage Command.*

USS *Ohio* in Dry Dock #2 at the Mare Island Navy Yard, c. 1914. The third *Ohio* (BB–12) was laid down April 22, 1899, by Union Iron Works, launched May 18, 1901, and commissioned October 4, 1904. Designated flagship of the Asiatic Fleet, *Ohio* departed San Francisco April 1, 1905. *Courtesy of the Naval History and Heritage Command.*

USS *Missouri* (BB-11) in dry dock at the Philadelphia Navy Yard, Pennsylvania, October 27, 1918, showing the paravane skeg attached to her forefoot. The *Missouri* recommissioned on April 23, 1917, shortly after the United States entered into World War I, where she joined the Atlantic Fleet at Yorktown, Virginia, and operated as a training ship in the Chesapeake Bay area for the duration of the war. *Courtesy of the Naval History and Heritage Command.*

The USS *Vandalia* fitting out in a dry dock at the Boston Navy Yard, Massachusetts, c. early 1876. Behind her, at right, is the USS *Adams*, and in the distance is the Navy Yard's receiving ship, USS *Ohio*. The Navy established five recruiting stations by the end of 1825 in Boston, New York, Philadelphia, Baltimore, and Norfolk. They operated only when seamen were needed and closed down as soon as manpower requirements were fulfilled. The Navy typically used receiving ships, which were stationed permanently in a main harbor, for the purpose of recruiting seamen and holding them until needed. *Courtesy of the Naval History and Heritage Command.*

Bow view of the USS *Intrepid*, showing a torpedo projection device at her forefoot, cradled in a dry dock at the Boston Navy Yard. She has a torpedo projection device at her forefoot, c. 1874. The second *Intrepid* was launched by the Boston Navy Yard on March 5, 1874, and eventually decommissioned and sold in 1892. *Courtesy of the Naval History and Heritage Command.*

View of Dry Dock Number 1 at the Mare Island Navy Yard, California, on March 7, 1914, showing the USRC *McCulloch* (U.S. Revenue Cutter) and two unidentified submarines. The dry dock was begun in 1872 and finished in 1891 for $2,772,332. Prior to the completion of Dry Dock Number 1, Mare Island used a floating dry dock to repair ships. *Courtesy of the U.S. Navy Seabee Museum.*

The USS *Justin* cradled in the Mare Island Navy Yard dry dock, c. 1899-1900. The first *Justin,* a schooner, was launched in 1891 by R. Dixon & Co., Middlesbrough, England. The Navy purchased her from Bowring & Archibald and commissioned her into the fleet April 27, 1898. The *Justin* performed collier services during the Spanish-American War. After visiting Brazil, Chile, Peru, and Mexico, she arrived in San Francisco February 3, 1899, and was decommissioned. *Courtesy of the Naval History and Heritage Command.*

View of part of the Puget Sound Naval Shipyard waterfront, March 8, 1926. The USS *Thompson* (DD-305) is tied up to the pier at left, with a work float alongside her. *Courtesy of the Naval History and Heritage Command.*

The USS *Cuttlefish* in Auxiliary Repair Dock 1 (ARD-1) at the Naval Operating Base, San Diego, California, October 3, 1935. In 1933, the ARD-1 (Auxiliary Repair Dock 1) was designed and built as the first mobile floating dry dock. A one-piece dock shaped as a ship in form, the ARD-1 had a molded closed bow, a stern gate, and was U-shaped. The dock was equipped with its own diesel electric power plant, pumping plant, repair shops, and crew accommodations. It was the first dry dock in the navy to be self-sustaining enough to accompany the fleet into remote waters. The ARD-1 had an overall length of 393 feet, beam 60 feet, light draft 5 feet, and a deep draft of 30 feet, depending on variable operating conditions. Additional facilities added to the ARD-1 included commander officer quarters, a room for one other officer, and 24 enlisted men (later expanded to 36 men); an oil burning range, electric refrigerators, and drinking fountains; washing and sanitary installations, bunks, mess tables, and benches; and lockers, desks, and other furniture and equipment

with towing gear, including duplicate hawser and with two whaleboats hung from suitable deck fittings. The USS *Cuttlefish*, an 1130-ton Cachalot class submarine built at Groton, Connecticut, was commissioned in June 1934 and, following initial service in the Atlantic area, she deployed to the Pacific in June 1935. When the Pacific war began in December 1941, the *Cuttlefish* was completing an overhaul at the Mare Island Navy Yard, California. Following her return to Pearl Harbor, she began her first war patrol in January 1942. After her third wartime cruise in the Pacific, she was ordered to the Atlantic for training service. Assigned to the Groton Submarine School, she spent the rest of World War II as a combat training tool for submarine officers and men. The USS *Cuttlefish* decommissioned in October 1945, and she was sold for scrap in February 1947. *Courtesy of the U.S. Navy Seabee Museum.*

The Dewey Floating Dry Dock (YFD-1) docked in the harbor at the Naval Station Olongapo, Philippine Islands, c. 1909. The Dewey floating steel dry dock, built by the Maryland Steel Company, was designed specifically to be towed to the Olongapo Naval Station. The self-docking, floating steel structure composed of sidewalls and pontoons could expand to five hundred feet in length, had a width of one hundred feet, and could raise a vessel of 16,000 gross tons. The Navy towed the dry dock to the Olongapo Naval Station by way of the Mediterranean Sea and the Suez Canal, a distance of 13,000 miles. The cost to tow the dry dock to the Philippines was $249,092, including pay and rations for officers and crew of the towing vessels and the U.S. Tug *Potomac*, which accompanied the dock to the Suez Canal. This also included the cost of canal tolls, as well as coal, water, and other stores consumed by the dry dock and towing vessels. The dock arrived in the Philippines July 9, 1909. Construction began April 1903 and finished June 1905 at a cost of $1,143,959. *Courtesy of the U.S. Navy Seabee Museum.*

View of the Dewey Floating Dry Docking at work at the U.S. Naval Station Olongapo, Philippine Islands, February 15, 1911. *Courtesy of the U.S. Navy Seabee Museum.*

Floating Dry Dock (YFD-2) at Algiers Naval Station, New Orleans, Louisiana, August 26, 1913. When Secretary Chandler restricted operation at the Pensacola Navy Yard in 1883, the possibility of a yard at New Orleans was investigated. Prior to the Civil War, the Navy purchased 23 acres of land in Algiers, Louisiana, just outside of New Orleans. The Navy maintained a small naval station at Algiers and later expanded it in 1893. In 1901, due to the rapid current and poor soil conditions, a floating dry dock, rather than a graving dry dock, was chosen to be added to the newly renamed New Orleans Naval Station. Built by the Maryland Steel Company of Baltimore, Maryland, the dry dock measured 525 feet by 126 feet and weighed six thousand tons. It could lift a vessel in three and a half hours and was capable of raising 15,000 tons six feet above the water and 18,000 tons with the deck flooded. *Courtesy of the U.S. Navy Seabee Museum.*

In order for smaller naval vessels to be taken economically and conveniently out of the water for repairs or overhauling, a marine railway was essential to the care of such vessels. The marine railway was often desirable at naval stations because of its economic operation and the urgent need of dry docks for major vessels. At a station where docks were not available, the marine railway became an indispensable requisite.

The marine railway became the first advanced technique developed to work on the hull of a ship and haul her out of water. Prior to this, ships needing hull repairs were hauled on shore at high tide and careened on their sides to expose half of the hull at a time. In 1822, Commodore John Rodgers built the first inclined marine railway in the United States at the Washington Navy Yard. The first ship was run up the railway through the power exerted on a 10" hawser, and the ship moved upwards at the rate of three feet per minute.

A marine railway included the construction of heavy rails on a solid foundation that extended into deep water. On the rails sat a wooden cradle onto which the ship floated. The ship was firmly braced to prevent lateral structural strain. On the bottom of the cradle were numerous rollers or wheels which fit onto the rails, allowing the whole cradle with the ship to be drawn up much more easily by man or animal power exerted on the capstans at the dock head. Originally men or horses would have been used to drag the cradle and vessel up the slipway, but with the advent of the steam engine, most marine railways were converted to steam powered operation. Later, electric or electro-hydraulic winches became standard.

USS *Delphy* hauled out on the marine railway at the Boston Navy Yard, 1919. The USS *Delphy* carried a 3"/23 anti-aircraft gun atop her after deckhouse and had no 4"/50 gun or depth charge racks fitted on her stern. The *Delphy* was the lead destroyer of seven that crashed on the rocks near Point Pedernales, California, in inclement weather on September 8, 1923. She collided broadside and broke in half, with her stern below the surface. Three men died and 15 were injured. The *Delphy* was decommissioned on October 26, 1923, and sold as a wreck October 19, 1925. *Courtesy of the Naval History and Heritage Command.*

View of the Boston Navy Yard marine railway from the northwest, May 5, 1919. Commodore John Rodgers invented the marine railway, which was designed to haul ships up to 2,000 tons displacement out of the water for repairs and maintenance. It was often constructed in conjunction with a shiphouse to protect the lifted vessel. In order for smaller naval vessels to be conveniently and economically taken out of the water for repairs or overhauling, a marine railway was essential to the care of such vessels. The marine railway was often desirable at naval stations because of its economic operation and the urgent need of dry docks for major vessels. At a station where docks were not available, the marine railway became an indispensable requisite. *Courtesy of the U.S. Navy Seabee Museum.*

The Charleston Navy Yard marine railway looking northeast, showing U.S. Tug *Sebago* on ways cradle about 3/4 way up, July 1, 1919. The second *Sebago,* a tug built in 1893 by John H. Dialogue and Son, was purchased for service during the Spanish-American War as *Hortense* from O'Connor and Smoot on April 30, 1898. Renamed *Sebago* in January 1900 and designated YT-23 in July 1920, the harbor tug remained in service at various stations, including Pensacola, Guantanamo Bay, Port Royal, Charleston, Norfolk, and Philadelphia, until struck from the Navy list on December 3, 1936. *Courtesy of the U.S. Navy Seabee Museum.*

General view of Marine Railway Number 1 at the Olongapo Naval Station, Philippines, September 2, 1913. According to the nameplate on the engine, the Spanish Navy constructed the marine railway in 1884. *Courtesy of the U.S. Navy Seabee Museum.*

Bow view of USCG *Ossipee* in the cradle during testing of the Boston Navy Yard marine railway, June 2, 1919. *Ossipee,* built by the Newport News Shipbuilding and Dry Dock Corporation as a cruising cutter, was launched in 1915. Commissioned on July 28, 1915, she arrived in Portland, Maine, on August 17, 1915, and commenced coastal patrol and rescue operations in a cruising district from Eastport, Maine, to Cape Ann, Massachusetts. The cutter cruised in the war zone from August 23, 1917, until November 11, 1918. Upon returning to the U.S., she resumed patrol and rescue operations out of Portland, Maine. *Courtesy of the U.S. Navy Seabee Museum.*

The Submarine USS *G-3* hauled out of water at the Lake Torpedo Boat Company shipyard, Bridgeport, Connecticut, December 9, 1915. *Turbot* (Submarine No. 31) was laid down on March 30, 1911, at Bridgeport, Connecticut, by the Lake Torpedo Boat Company. She was renamed *G-3* on November 17, 1911. Following the cancellation of the Lake Torpedo Boat contract, she was transferred to the New York Navy Yard for completion on November 17, 1913. She was launched on December 27, 1913, and commissioned at the New York Navy Yard on March 22, 1915. *Courtesy of the Naval History and Heritage Command.*

On March 27, 1794, President George Washington signed a bill authorizing the construction of six famous frigates, the *Constitution*, *Constellation*, *United States*, *President*, *Chesapeake*, and *Congress*, to defend U.S. merchant ships against Algerian pirates. While these frigates were very different from the ships and carriers of today's Navy, they nonetheless represent the initial force of the Navy's current global force.

Before completion of the frigates, the United States signed a treaty with Algiers and the bill authorizing ship construction was suspended. However the president, reluctant to lose the frigates, continued construction with the justification that to stop work suddenly would not be in the best financial interest of the communities involved.

Building ships for the U.S. Navy at Hog Island, Pennsylvania, April 29, 1918. In 1917, as part of the World War I effort, the U.S. government contracted American International Shipbuilding to build ships and a shipyard at Hog Island. At the time, Hog Island was the largest shipyard in the world with 50 slipways. *Courtesy of the National Archives.*

USS *Craven* (Destroyer #70) under construction at the Norfolk Navy Yard, Portsmouth, Virginia, December 11, 1917. View looks forward from over the stern and shows framing and bulkheads in place. Her keel was laid November 20, 1917, and she launched June 29, 1918. *Courtesy of the Naval History and Heritage Command.*

Chapter 3: Shipbuilding

Photograph of Shipbuilding Ways Number 2 looking south at the Philadelphia Navy Yard, Pennsylvania, April 13, 1938. World War I led to the extensive expansion of every corner of League Island, including Shipbuilding Ways Number 2 and 3. A large part of the Bureau of Yards and Docks activities for the war included improving and equipping the various navy yards for the construction of vessels. *Courtesy of the U.S. Navy Seabee Museum.*

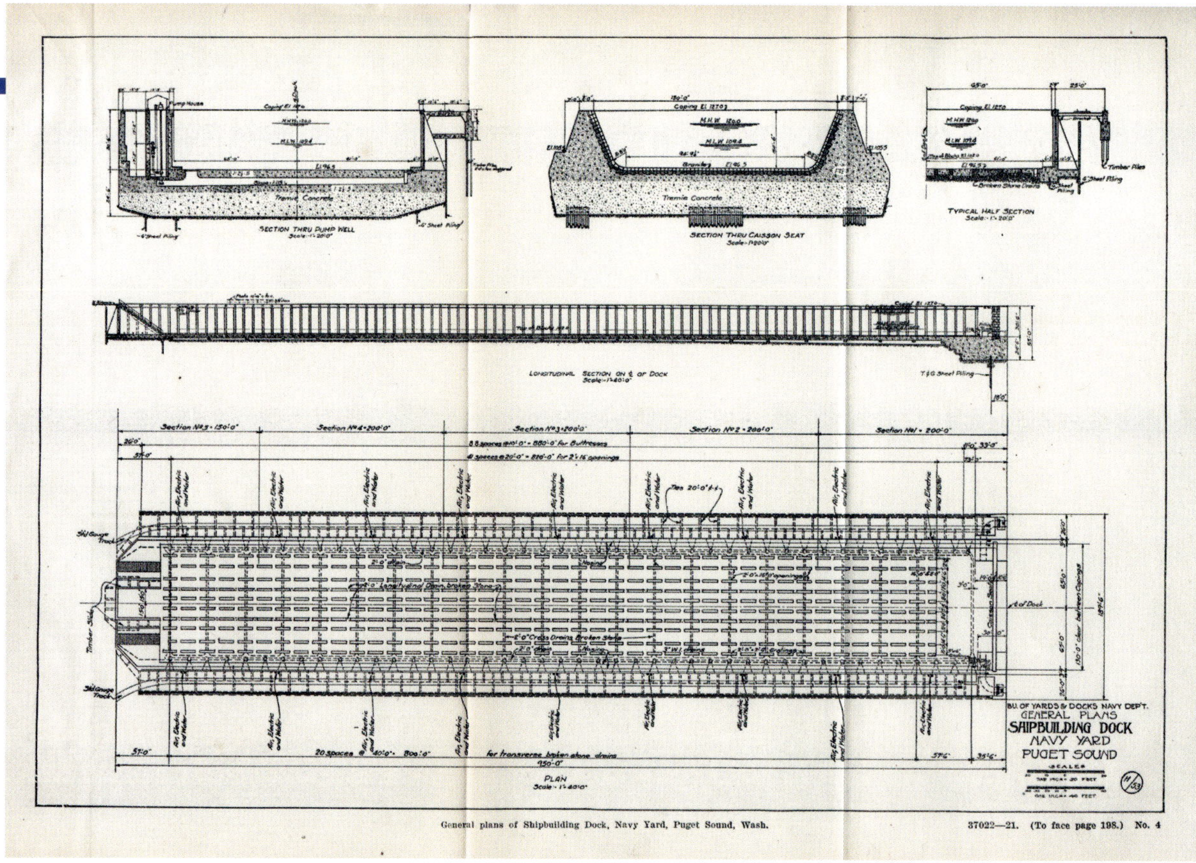

General plans for Shipbuilding Docks at the Puget Sound Naval Shipyard, 1917. The most striking departure from the customary practice found in the Bureau's entire program of World War I shipbuilding facilities was the construction of a shallow dry dock in lieu of the usual building ways. *Courtesy of the U.S. Navy Seabee Museum*

Supply Ship #1 under construction at the Boston Navy Yard, showing the inner bottom framing looking forward, June 30, 1915. The shipbuilding ways at navy yards were designed in accordance to the requirements of the Bureau of Construction and Repair, while also taking into account the specific issues of each location as to foundation conditions, available space, and tide ranges. *Courtesy of the U.S. Navy Seabee Museum.*

Photograph of the shipbuilding facility while under construction at the Puget Sound Naval Shipyard, Washington, June 1, 1918. View from the head end of the dock, showing forms looking northwest. In a departure from the customary shipbuilding facilities, the Bureau of Yards and Docks constructed the country's first shallow dry dock for shipbuilding purposes at the Puget Sound Naval Shipyard. The dock was designed and constructed 130 feet wide, 928 feet long, and 20 feet deep. *Courtesy of the National Archives.*

View of the shipbuilding ways at the Boston Navy Yard, from the southeast, March 12, 1915. The Crandall Engineering Company designed and built the ways. *Courtesy of the U.S. Navy Seabee Museum.*

Photograph of the Boston Navy Yard shipbuilding ways from the southeast, April 15, 1915. In 1913, the Board of Inspectors for Shore Stations recommended the addition of a 450-foot building way to construct fleet auxiliaries. The ways, devoted to the construction and launching of vessels, were designed in accordance with the requirements of the Bureau of Construction and Repair. *Courtesy of the U.S. Navy Seabee Museum.*

Boston Navy Yard shipbuilding ways on June 1, 1915, showing four shipbuilding cranes installed under contract. During World War I, the shipbuilding facilities at the navy yard were used to construct one store ship, three tankers, and a destroyer tender. *Courtesy of the U.S. Navy Seabee Museum.*

Three of the frigates – the *Constitution* in Boston, the *United States* in Philadelphia, and the *Constellation* in Baltimore – were completed, while work on the other three stopped and perishable materials were sold.

The first action taken on the establishment of permanent navy yards occurred under the first Secretary of the Navy, Benjamin Stoddert (1798-1801). Although Congress had repeatedly refused the Navy Department's specific request to purchase land for a shipyard, Stoddert obtained authority through a liberal interpretation of the law, in which Congress appropriated money for construction of six 74-gun frigates. At the time, the Navy rented space at yards that were too small for the newly authorized ships. Since it was not within the best interest of the government to improve private property, President Adams and Secretary Stoddert agreed to purchase land for building navy yards.

The first six navy yards were located at Portsmouth, New Hampshire; Brooklyn, New York; Washington, District of Columbia; Gosport, Virginia; Charlestown, Massachusetts; and Philadelphia, Pennsylvania. Selection and purchase of the land was completed in record time. Stoddert feared the incoming president, Thomas Jefferson, would undo all his work if the business failed to be completed prior to his taking office. By the time Stoddert completed his term as Secretary the purchases were virtually completed.

Thomas Jefferson, who believed the country had invested too much in naval development, justified Stoddert's fear and swore to reduce naval spending to the lowest terms possible. Jefferson leaned towards fewer navy yards and fewer, smaller ships, rather than the larger 74-gun frigates. Although he doubted the legality of the land purchases and called for an investigation to determine exactly how many

View on the main deck of the USS *Craven* (Destroyer #70) looking from amidships while she was under construction at the Norfolk Navy Yard, Portsmouth, Virginia, June 4, 1918. Prior to World War I, only two yards had adequate facilities to build large battleships. With plans to construct cruisers over 200 feet longer than any other previous battleship, plans were started to remodel and extend building ways already available. *Courtesy of the Naval History and Heritage Command.*

Photograph of the USS *New York* keel laying at the New York Navy Yard shipbuilding ways, c. 1911. The fifth *New York* (BB–34) was laid down September 11, 1911, at the New York Navy Yard; she launched on October 30, 1912; and was commissioned April 15, 1914. *Courtesy of the Library of Congress, George Grantham Bain Collection.*

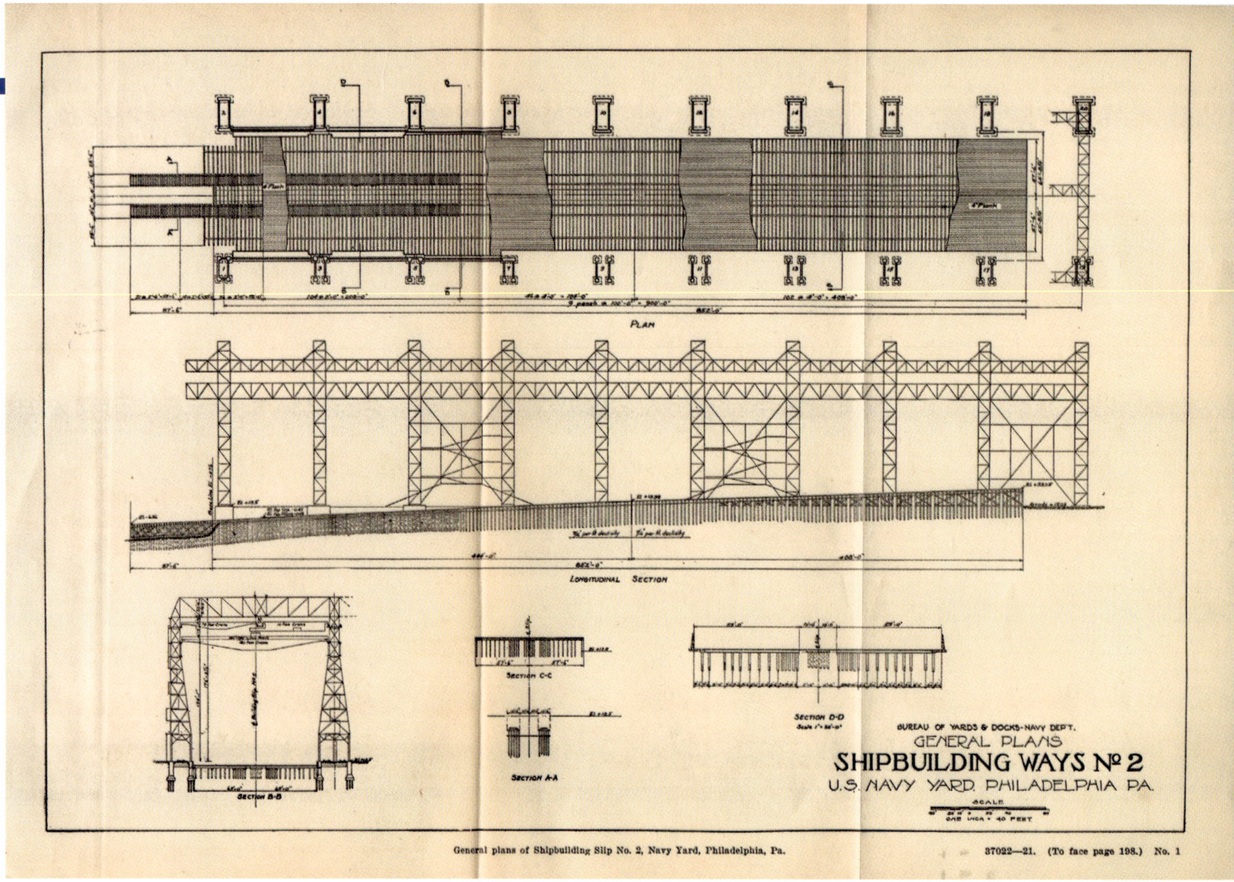

General plans for Shipbuilding Ways Number 2 at the Philadelphia Navy Yard, Pennsylvania, 1917. *Courtesy of the U.S. Navy Seabee Museum*

yards were necessary, in the end, the Navy maintained the original six yards. Ironically, for a man so against military spending Jefferson's terms underwent years of conflict, including a war with Tripoli, a war with Spain looming throughout, and a second war with Great Britain seeming inevitable.

In the age of sail, shipyard executives came from the ranks of artisans and naval architects from the ranks of draftsmen. The industry ran on practical experience and on the results of past performance. In 1794, George Washington hired six civilian constructors to oversee the construction of each of the first six frigates. The naval constructor at Philadelphia was named "Principal Constructor of the Navy." In 1836, the Navy appointed the first naval marine engineer as a civilian and soon regulated the position, tightening relations with line officers.

When the Navy ordered a new ship built or extensive repairs be made to an old ship at a Navy yard, a Naval Constructor, working for the Bureau of Construction and Repair, was employed to supervise the work. When the work was completed, the Navy often laid off the Naval Constructor until further work was needed. In 1866, Congress authorized the establishment of the Corps of Naval Constructors, providing permanent status for the Navy's marine engineers. However, they were given the same relative rank and recognition that had been gained over the years by the Medical Corps, Civil Engineer Corps, and Pursers, which was not without considerable difficulty and controversy.

General view of Shipbuilding Ways Number 1 and 4 at the New York Navy Yard, November 1, 1920. In the early 1900s, Shipbuilding Ways Number 1 was rebuilt to facilitate construction of the first class battleships on the drawing board. In 1903 the yard began constructing the USS *Connecticut*, the first in a new breed of warships. *Courtesy of the U.S. Navy Seabee Museum.*

USS *Maryland* (Armored Cruiser #8) being prepared for launching at the Newport News Shipbuilding and Dry Dock Company shipyard, Newport News, Virginia, shortly before she launched on September 12, 1903. In October 1905, the *Maryland* joined the Atlantic Fleet for operations along the east coast and in the Caribbean, where she took part in the 1906 winter maneuvers off Cuba. *Courtesy of the Naval History and Heritage Command, Mary M. Galt Collection.*

A 20-ton locomotive gantry crane designed around Dry Dock Number 3 at the Puget Sound Naval Shipyard, 1936. The revolving structure mounted on a tower allowed standard gauge rolling stock on tracks to pass underneath. *Courtesy of the U.S. Navy Seabee Museum.*

In 1842, the Navy established five Bureaus to disseminate the naval authority of the Secretary. One of those established was the Bureau of Construction, Equipment, and Repair, with responsibilities for designing, building, outfitting, and equipping naval ships. A Chief Naval Constructor, who was independent of all the rest of the Bureaus, headed the newly created Bureau. When the Navy ordered a ship constructed, naval leaders decided the number and size of the guns she was to carry. However, the Chief Naval Constructor chose her model and design, making him responsible for her dependable and accurate construction.

In 1862, when the Navy reorganized, the five original Bureaus were separated into eight. As a result, the Bureau of Construction, Equipment, and Repair separated into three Bureaus: Construction and Repair; Equipment and Recruiting; and Steam Engineering. The Bureau's name "Construction and Repair" indicated the two main branches of work. Each of these branches was under the direct charge of a Naval Constructor. The first is essentially a shipbuilding branch, and dealt primarily outside of the Bureau with private shipyards or navy yards where vessels were under construction. The second was a maintenance division, which dealt primarily outside of the Bureau with the navy yards and vessels of the fleet.

This reorganization adversely affected the Navy's shipbuilding capabilities, but while they quickly realized the adverse effects, it did not become critical until the large shipbuilding resurgence of the 1880s. The fundamental idea of having each Bureau system remain independent and able to carry out its duties without interference between Bureaus was not realized in practice. This was largely due to the distribution of duties between Bureaus being more or less irregular and illogical. The Navy Department occasionally supplemented the specific requirements assigned to and the cognizance of the Bureau of Construction and Repair. Shipbuilding troubles arising from this renaissance generated a string of Bureau consolidations and reorganizations that continued until 1940.

American naval development, both in numbers and design of ships, lagged until the mid-1880s, when Congress sponsored a sizeable shipbuilding program to modernize the fleet. These new ships required large quantities of advanced ordnance. In 1886, the Secretary of the Navy issued an order demanding increased facilities to construct canons and other ordnance for use on the new iron-hull ships of war. This included the reassignment of shops and buildings at the Washington Navy Yard to the control of the Bureau of Ordnance.

USS *Turbot* (Submarine #31) under construction at the Lake Torpedo Boat Company shipyard, Bridgeport, Connecticut, September 28, 1911. The *Turbot* was renamed G-3 in November 1911, prior to the cancellation of the Lake Torpedo Boat contract. The *Turbot* transferred to the New York Navy Yard for completion on November 17, 1913, and launched on December 27, 1913. *Courtesy of the Naval History and Heritage Command.*

The *V-5* submarine half finished at the Portsmouth Navy Yard, 1927. The USS *Narwhal* (SS-167), the lead ship of her class of submarine and one of the "V-boats," was the second ship of the United States Navy to be named for the Narwhal. She was designated V-5 (SC-1) when her keel was laid down on May 10, 1927, at the Portsmouth Navy Yard, Maine. *Courtesy of the U.S. Navy.*

Photograph showing construction of shipbuilding facilities in accordance with the Bureau of Construction and Repair requirements at the Charleston Navy Yard, South Carolina, looking east, February 15, 1934. The Civil Works Administration (CWA) and the National Industrial Recovery Act (NIRA) funded the project as part of their program to get citizens back to work. *Courtesy of the U.S. Navy Seabee Museum.*

View of the New York Navy Yard's new 350-ton hammerhead crane erected near Berth 12, June 4, 1940. This photograph was taken before construction of the tower house between the B and C levels of the octagonal tower. Because of the Hepburn Report, industrial facilities were increased at all bases and numerous cranes were purchased and placed in operation at all stations. *Courtesy of the U.S. Navy Seabee Museum.*

Navy personnel inspect the USS *Von Steuben* crew at the Philadelphia Navy Yard, Pennsylvania, August 4, 1917. The tents were the crew's berthing quarters while their ship was being outfitted for U.S. Navy service. After the United States declared war on the German Empire, the *Kronprinz Wilhelm,* later renamed the *Von Steuben*, was seized while in port in Philadelphia. On May 22nd, President Wilson issued the executive order which authorized the Navy to take possession of the ship and begin repairs. In the summer of 1917, the *Von Steuben* began her Navy career as an auxiliary cruiser. *Courtesy of the Naval History and Heritage Command.*

Towing Target Number 48 launches at the Philadelphia Navy Yard, Pennsylvania, on August 5, 1918. The transport USS *Henderson* is in the background. *Courtesy of the Naval History and Heritage Command.*

Launch of the U.S. Navy submarine *Snapper* at the Fore River Works in Quincy, Massachusetts, June 6, 1909. The first *Snapper* (SS-16) was renamed *C-5* on November 17, 1911. *Snapper*, an early gasoline-engine submarine, took part in early efforts to develop tactical concepts for the burgeoning submarine Navy. *Courtesy of the Library of Congress.*

USS *L-8* (Submarine #48) under construction inside the Franklin Shiphouse at the Portsmouth Navy Yard, Maine, April 13, 1916. L-8 (SS-48) was laid down February 24, 1915, at the Portsmouth Navy Yard; she launched April 23, 1917; and was commissioned August 30, 1917. Following training operations along the east coast, L-8 prepared for European service. *Courtesy of the Naval History and Heritage Command.*

USS *Constitution,* later renamed the USS *Lexington* (CV-2), under construction at the Philadelphia Navy Yard, Pennsylvania, July 14, 1921. Photographed by Replugle, looking aft from the bow area with the bulkhead frame 75 in the center. In 1920, the United States had declared an aim to produce a navy "second to none," and had already laid down keels for five battleships and four battle cruisers. In February 1922, the Washington Naval Limitations Treaty, also known as the Five-Power Treaty of 1922, halted construction of this ship. Following the Washington Naval Conference, the USS *Lexington* and the USS *Saratoga* were both re-designated and reauthorized to be completed as aircraft carriers on July 1, 1922. *Courtesy of the Naval History and Heritage Command.*

Since the early 1800s, the Navy had followed a policy of contracting most of its shipbuilding to private contractors. This cost saving practice had under prepared the Navy's shipyards for the huge shipbuilding and ship repair requirements dictated by the First World War. Improvements to building facilities and repair facilities started with the improvement and equipage of the navy yards at Puget Sound, Philadelphia, Norfolk, New York, Boston, Portsmouth, Charleston, and New Orleans for the construction of ships.

By the mid-1920s, the size and weight of naval vessels, as well as the variety of conditions at the navy yards where ships were built and repaired, necessitated new developments in the design and construction of shipbuilding and repair plants, including shops, building slips, and dry docks. This also required special types for outfitting, repair, and replacement service.

Shipbuilders build vessels, except in rare cases, upon an inclined plane or "way," so that at the proper time they are released to slip into the water under natural forces. Important progress had been made in the design and construction of such shipbuilding ways for the Navy by 1925, both in type and in details of construction, particularly in the provision of crane service and in the use of both timber and permanent reinforced-concrete construction.

Keel laying of the USS *S-5* (Submarine #110) at the Portsmouth Navy Yard, Maine, December 4, 1917. The *S-5* launched on November 10, 1919, and was commissioned on March 6, 1920. *Courtesy of the Naval History and Heritage Command.*

USS *S-3* (Submarine #107) slides into the water during her launching at the Portsmouth Navy Yard, Maine, December 21, 1918. *S-3* was the third of the three original S-boats built by different contractors for performance comparison. Each builder was allowed to create their own individual designs, but were required to follow the same general performance criteria. *S-1* was known as the "Holland-type," *S-2* as the "Lake-type," and *S-3* as the "Government-type." *Courtesy of the Naval History and Heritage Command.*

View of Shipbuilding Way Number 2 at the Boston Navy Yard from Crane #3 looking northwest, May 2, 1934. In 1933, the yard was designated as a building facility for destroyers and small craft. In order to facilitate this designation the yard built a second shipbuilding ways. *Courtesy of the U.S. Navy Seabee Museum.*

USS *California* (BB-44) launching ceremony, showing the bow view looking down the ways to the stern, on the ways at Mare Island Navy Yard, November 20, 1919. For 20 years (1921-1941), *California* served first as flagship of the Pacific Fleet, then as flagship of the Battle Fleet (Battle Force), U.S. Fleet. *Courtesy of the National Archives.*

The Navy's most important departure from the customary shipbuilding practice was the construction of a shallow dry dock for ship construction instead of the usual launching ways at the Puget Sound Navy Yard. Conditions were found favorable at the Navy yard, the tidal range being great and the firm and impervious geological formation permitting light walls and floor. In this construction, the ship was built on an even keel, making structural and mechanical installations relatively simple. The whole work is at a lower level than it would be on ways, making for greater accessibility and a lesser expenditure of human and mechanical energy. The vessel could then be much closer to completion before launching, and the risk and expense involved in the usual launching was then avoided. The dock was simply flooded, the ship floated, the caisson gate was removed, and the ship towed out.

In 1930, the Bureau of Construction and Repair and the Bureau of Engineering each had major responsibilities in connection with the design, construction, maintenance, and repair of ships. Some of these responsibilities were also assigned to the Bureau of Ordnance and the Bureau of Navigation. Construction of individual ships was authorized in a piecemeal basis, and no one agency had complete charge of the overall coordination of the building scope.

The Vinson-Trammell Act of 1934 authorized the expansion of the fleet and the replacement of overage vessels decommissioned as part of the Washington and London Treaties of 1922. In 1930, the Navy owned nine naval shipyards, one industrial naval station, and three laboratories. There were no Navy-owned facilities at private plants. It soon became apparent under wartime pressure that the U.S. could mobilize and train forces faster than it could produce weapons and equipment needed. Consequently, a great expansion of the Navy-owned shore facilities, supplemented by construction of facilities at private plants, was undertaken.

Workers extend Shipbuilding Ways Number 2 at the New York Navy Yard, looking east showing the completed steelwork, January 31, 1940. Shipbuilding Ways Number 2 were completely reconstructed with WPA funds and Navy contract. The Bureau of Yards and Docks strengthened and expanded the ways to enable them to build and repair the new Iowa class battleships. The Navy extended the shipways crane structure and new 50-ton cranes were installed. *Courtesy of the U.S. Navy Seabee Museum.*

To expedite the construction of ships for the fleet, government-funded extensions were made at private shipbuilder plants and machinery manufacturers. The Bureau of Yards and Docks' shipyard plants division designed the layout plans for 235 private yards that held contracts for emergency fleet corporation vessels. The extensions were classed in three general groups: facilities that remained the property of the contractor; plants whereby some or all of the additions could be taken over by the contractor at market value; or rentals that the government defrayed the entire cost of and, later, remained the property of the government. Thirty-four forging plants were engaged in the construction of torpedo-boat destroyers, scout cruisers, submarines, minesweepers, and accessories for these vessels. Two plants provided coal storage; one produced airplane propellers; and eight produced shafting and ordnance material.

A series of problems with the vital pre-World War II shipbuilding programs occurred in 1939, providing the impetus that caused the merging of the Bureaus of Construction and Repair and Engineering to form the Bureau of Ships in 1940. Serious shipbuilding delays had inevitably come about due to two recurring factors: inter-Bureau disputes concerning technical cognizance and minimal cooperation in areas that demanded the most understanding of balancing design, production, and material delivery considerations.

Shipbuilding ways being demolished at the Charleston Navy Yard, South Carolina, April 8, 1931. The disarmament treaties of the 1920s ironically contributed to the rearmament of the fleet in the 1930s. The number of warships had fallen well below the number authorized, motivating the Navy to decide to rebuild to treaty strength. This encouraged Congress to also pass a dry dock bill and appropriate funds to rebuild the shipbuilding ways at many of the navy yards, including the ones at the Charleston Navy Yard. *Courtesy of the U.S. Navy Seabee Museum.*

Photograph of the caisson under construction for the new shipbuilding dry dock at the Puget Sound Naval Shipyard, August 14, 1918. The Bureau of Yards and Docks departed from its customary practice of shipbuilding facilities by constructing a shallow dry dock at Puget Sound in lieu of the standard shipbuilding ways. *Courtesy of the National Archives.*

By 1940, the Navy began extensive progress towards improving and extending shipbuilding facilities at all the industrial navy yards. These were urgently needed to provide for repair and new construction. Appurtenant industrial facilities were being provided at all yards to meet the increased load upon the shore establishment for the repair and improvement of vessels. The Navy added important facilities at the naval dry dock, South Boston, to affect repairs to ships undergoing overhaul in that dock.

Provision of these new facilities and expansion of the old ones resulted in bringing capacity for construction and repair to levels which permitted the successful construction and support of the vastly expanded fleet required to win World War II, and for carrying on the research necessary to insure obtaining the best technical equipment possible. Those facilities were capable of supporting the fleet against any foreseeable enemy, helped the U.S. win the war, and were major factors in assisting the U.S. reach its current global status.

Five children and their nanny sitting outside the ropewalk at the Boston Navy Yard, Anchor Park, Rope Walk Avenue, 1890. The Navy had an extensive need for hemp and sisal products as lines, halliards, hawsers, and ropes, which were supplied by commercial manufacturers from 1800-1830. However, the necessity for heavier hawsers for warships than those manufactured for commercial vessels led the Navy to create its own ropewalks at specialized shops in several navy yards. Boston, New York, and Memphis had the largest comprehensive ropewalk complexes. The name ropewalk derived from the constant walking back and forth of the workers involved in the hand spinning of cord fibers. Towards the close of 1831, the Board of Navy Commissioners informed Commandant Morris of the Boston Navy Yard that they intended to submit to Congress a proposition to build two ropewalks. The Board requested information in order to build the ropewalks and cost estimates for the necessary fireproof buildings. In the spring of 1835, $50,000 was appropriated to begin construction of the ropewalk complex at the Boston Navy Yard, which would include a 70- by 60-foot three-story head house and basement; a 200- by 19-foot tarring house; and a two story hemp house. In the head building, the necessary partitions were placed to accommodate the steam engine and other machinery. A major importance was placed on having the steam machinery, boilers, and fires enclosed far away from the hemp to prohibit any fire or other danger to the rest of the complex. The outside of the Boston ropewalk was made of Quincy granite, filled with brick and mortar, with no other woodwork and a roof covered with large slate to make it fireproof. *Courtesy of the Naval History and Heritage Command.*

Rope Layer at the Boston Navy Yard Ropewalk, c. 1905. The machines used to spin hemp could spin up to 1,000 tons of tarred cordage annually. *Courtesy of the National Park Service.*

Top cart and rope hauler at the Boston Navy Yard Ropewalk, c. 1905. A ropewalk is a long straight narrow lane, or a covered pathway, where long strands of hemp could be combed out through a series of steel prongs and laid out before being twisted into rope. The principal of the walk is that yarns are stretched out between revolving hooks, often 300 yards apart, and these hooks twist the yarns together. *Courtesy of the National Park Service.*

Forming cart at the Boston Navy Yard Ropewalk, c. 1905. *Courtesy of the National Park Service.*

During the Navy's first two decades, commercial manufacturers supplied the hemp and sisal products used as lines, halliards, hawsers, and ropes. However, the necessity for heavier hawsers for warships than those manufactured for commercial vessels led the Navy to create its own ropewalks as specialized shops at several navy yards. Boston, New York, and Memphis had the largest comprehensive ropewalk complexes. The name ropewalk derived from the constant walking back and forth of the workers involved in the hand spinning of cord fibers.

Towards the close of 1831, the Board of Navy Commissioners informed Commandant Morris at the Boston Navy Yard that they intended to submit to Congress a proposition to build two ropewalks. The Board requested information in order to build the ropewalks and cost estimates for the necessary fireproof buildings.

Rope layer at the Boston Navy Yard Ropewalk, c. 1905. *Courtesy of the National Park Service.*

In the spring of 1835, the Navy appropriated $50,000 to begin construction of the ropewalk complex at the Boston Navy Yard that would include a 70- by 60-foot three-story head house and basement; a 200- by 19-foot-tarring house; and a two story hemp house. In the head building, the necessary partitions were placed to accommodate the steam engine and other machinery. A major importance was placed on having the steam machinery, boilers, and fires enclosed far away from the hemp to prohibit any fire or other danger to the rest of the complex. The outside of the Boston ropewalk was made of Quincy granite filled with brick and mortar, with no other woodwork, and a roof covered with large slate to make it fireproof.

Interior view of the laying room at the Boston Navy Yard Ropewalk, c. 1905. The name ropewalk was derived from the constant walking back and forth of the workers involved in the hand-spinning of cord fibers. The ropewalk complex included several structures. One building received and hackled fibers, another was used for spinning fibers into yard and roping, and facilities for oiling and tarring were required to complete the rope making process. *Courtesy of the National Park Service.*

View of the Franklin Shiphouse, Portsmouth Navy Yard, Maine, from the waterfront, May 18, 1922. The first necessity of any navy yard was to have wharves that were used for tying up ships undergoing minor dockside repairs, waiting for their turns upon the marine railways, graving or floating dry docks, or tied up. Shiphouses were built over the ways to protect workers and ships from inclement weather. *Courtesy of the U.S. Navy Seabee Museum.*

View of the shiphouse at the Washington Navy Yard, c. 1867. The waterfront area of the Washington Navy Yard was dominated by two big wooden shiphouses: one oriented roughly east west near the western end of the yard, the other running north south at the eastern end. *Courtesy of the Library of Congress.*

Launching of the USS *Maine* at the New York Navy Yard, November 18, 1889. Engraving from *Scientific American* magazine, Vol. 45, 1898. *Courtesy of the Naval History and Heritage Command.*

Shiphouses were huge hangar-like covered structures that provided shelter for ships during an overhaul, or when laid up "in ordinary." They were tall enough to dry dock the entire ship less the top section of the masts. On August 21, 1813, Commodore William Bainbridge proposed to construct houses over the ship's ways under construction at Charlestown, Massachusetts, and Portsmouth, New Hampshire. The workers, once protected, could not only work with more speed, but with more "neatness and efficiency." The shiphouse built over the ways at the Charlestown Navy Yard covered the *Independence* while under construction. It was the first of its kind ever erected.

At the navy yards at Charlestown (Boston), Portsmouth, Washington, and Brooklyn, these shiphouses were especially necessary to perform repair work during installation of overhead labor saving block and tackle equipment for weight lifting. Protection from the weather not only facilitated the work during construction, but also, if the ships were retained for any period on the stocks, added greatly to the durability of the ship after completion. Soon shiphouses were part of every Navy yard. By 1850 Boston had four shiphouses, and the other yards had at least two each.

View of the shiphouses at the Boston Navy Yard, 1928. The Navy's first shiphouse, completed in 1814, was constructed at the Boston Navy Yard over the shipways to protect ships and staff from the weather. By 1850, Boston had four shiphouses and two building slips; Philadelphia had two shiphouses; and the other main yards had at least two each. *Courtesy of the U.S. Navy Seabee Museum.*

View of the waterfront at the Boston Navy Yard, Charlestown, Massachusetts, from East Boston, c. 1876. Ships at left are the USS *Wabash*, outboard, with the USS *Niagara* housed inboard of her. The USS *Iowa* (ex-*Ammonoosuc*) is inboard of *Niagara*, with only her four smokestacks and stern visible. The large ships on the building ways in the center and extreme right are USS *Connecticut* (ex-*Pompanoosuc*) and USS *Pennsylvania* (ex-*Kewaydin*). *Courtesy of the Naval Historical Foundation*

Photograph of the Franklin Shiphouse at the Portsmouth Navy Yard, Maine, September 18, 1913. *Courtesy of the U.S. Navy Seabee Museum.*

Washington Navy Yard's eastern Shiphouse and marine railway, c. 1860s-'70s. *Courtesy of the Naval History and Heritage Command.*

Driving pile for the foundations of the experimental model basin at the Washington Navy Yard, February 1897. The old Washington Navy Yard shiphouse is on the right. *Courtesy of the U.S. Navy Seabee Museum.*

Photograph of the Franklin Shiphouse on fire the morning of March 10, 1936. On the morning of March 10, 1936, the Franklin Shiphouse burned down in a fiery pyre of flames and smoke. Unable to stop the fire, residents and naval personnel watched in vain as the historic shiphouse burned to the ground. *Courtesy of the U.S. Navy Seabee Museum.*

View of the Franklin Shiphouse after the fire. Photograph of the shiphouse ruins taken March 13, 1936, by public works personnel for the Bureau of Yards and Docks. *Courtesy of the U.S. Navy Seabee Museum.*

Interior view of the Franklin Shiphouse, Portsmouth Navy Yard, Maine, September 18, 1913. The Franklin Shiphouse was completed in 1838, stood 240 feet long, 131 feet wide, and 72 feet at its ridgepole. One hundred thirty tons of slate covered the roof, and it was considered the largest shiphouse in America. *Courtesy of the U.S. Navy Seabee Museum.*

Workers pave Central Avenue with asphalted wood blocks on 6-inch concrete foundation at the Mare Island Navy Yard, December 22, 1899. This is an early cyanotype image of the Mare Island Navy Yard. *Courtesy of the National Archives.*

Chapter 4: Public Works

Photograph of Locomotive #14 at the New York Navy Yard, 1918. Locomotives were first introduced to the navy yards in the mid-nineteenth century to ferry supplies and debris around the yard. *Courtesy of the U.S. Navy Seabee Museum.*

Street cleaning dump cart at the New York Navy Yard, April 3, 1919. Part of a street cleaner's daily tasks not only included picking up debris and trash, but also cleaning up after the many horses, oxen, and mules used at Navy bases until the 1930s. *Courtesy of the U.S. Navy Seabee Museum.*

The Bureau of Yards and Docks managed and administered all the shore construction, known as public works, for the Navy Department. Building construction, water, electricity, gas, telephone, sewerage, and trash disposal remain as essential to the operation of the Navy as they are to the resident of any town. The public works of the Navy comprises practically all construction, utilities, and maintenance at a Navy facility, such as shipbuilding facilities, transportation, and structures for every purpose needed by the Navy.

Until 1815, administrative control of the ever expanding shore establishment remained the sole responsibility of the Secretary of the Navy. On February 7, 1815, the scope of the work had expanded beyond his control, so the Secretary delegated authority to the newly created Board of Commissioners to be responsible for the building and maintaining of ships and managing the navy yards. The board also controlled procurement of Navy stores and materials; oversaw the construction, armament, equipment, and employment of vessels; and furnished accounts of Navy expenditures. However, the Navy continued to grow in size, technical complexity, and strength, causing the Board of Commissioners to become incapable of handling the job. In 1842, the Secretary of the Navy created a Bureau system with five branches to manage the various functions within the Navy.

With the creation of the Bureau system, the Navy vested the new Bureau of Navy Yards and Docks with the construction and maintenance of the docks, wharves, and buildings within the navy yards and stations. The Navy Department also gave the Bureau general control of the administration of the yards, control of timber

Commissioning ceremony for YM-12 *Endicott*, an electric hydraulic dredge at the Mare Island Navy Yard, California, December 11, 1926. The dredge was named for Rear Admiral Mordecai Endicott, the first Civil Engineer Corps officer to become Chief of the Bureau of Yards and Docks. *Courtesy of the U.S. Navy Seabee Museum.*

agents in the Southern States, and, in 1849, control of the Naval Asylum. In addition, the Bureau of Navy Yards and Docks provided basic maintenance labor for cleaning naval stations and watchmen for the protection of public property, except at those places directly under the cognizance of another Bureau or office. This included the care of the streets and grounds; removal of yard and ship refuse; furnishing of clerical and technical services; providing supplies for offices of the Commandant, Captain of the Yard, and Public Works Officer; and office supplies for Receiving Ship Offices on shore.

The naval shore establishment grew significantly between the creation of the Bureau system and the Civil War. The Navy established the Memphis Naval Station in 1844 to defend Americans living in the nation's interior near large inland waterways. During this time period, most of the navy yards underwent essential construction to maintain the buildings and keep up with new industrial inventions, including gas works, railroads, and steam run tools. In the 1840s, base improvements began at the Pensacola Navy Yard because of its strategic position on the Gulf Coast. In order to help the yard become a center for shipbuilding in the South, the Navy constructed a graving dock and the essential shops and plants.

Horse drawn fire engine at Building 99, Mare Island Navy Yard, October 18, 1914. Fire protection was a fundamental necessity at all navy yards. Steam fire engines later replaced the old hand pumping engines, which were state of the art for the era. *Courtesy of Library of Congress, Historic American Buildings Survey Collection.*

U.S. Helium Production Plant located in North Fort Worth, Texas, c. 1917. As a result of a natural gas field survey by the Bureau of Mines, the Navy Department contracted with the Lone Star Company to extract helium from natural gas for use in Navy lighter-than-air aircraft. *Courtesy of the U.S. Navy Seabee Museum.*

Foam fire protection system, solution tanks, and pump house looking from the southwest, January 6, 1919. Where no existing water supply was available at navy yards, elevated tanks were used to provide fire protection for automatic sprinkler systems. *Courtesy of the U.S. Navy Seabee Museum.*

At Boston in the late 1850s, naval engineers designed and constructed a steam-engineered building in the shape of a parallelogram. The facility housed a brass and iron foundry, a boiler shop, a blacksmith, and a machine shop in order to make the yard more self-sufficient. The boiler house and chimney were located at the center and contained eight boilers operating in pairs with five donkey pumps. The building also housed two one-hundred horsepower engines to power the complex.

In 1848, the New York Navy Yard added eighty additional acres of land to extend the burgeoning yard. The Bureau completed building new iron and copper storage, a quay wall, and dredging channels. They also paved streets, installed gutters and sewers, and constructed the commander's house in 1851. The Philadelphia yard improved the waterfront area, the channel to the yard was deepened, and the wharves extended. A new steam hammer and mooring anchors for the floating dry dock were installed in 1854, and extensions and repairs to the shiphouse were completed. This level of construction was being completed at most of the main navy yards, however, the sums received from Congress were always well below those requested, causing a stall in project completion.

Laborers install a new roof on a timber shed, Building 15(B) at the New York Navy Yard, view looking northwest, November 2, 1914. The timber shed was used to house pieces of timber used to compose the frame of a ship, including floor, futtock, and top timbers. *Courtesy of the U.S. Navy Seabee Museum.*

Both the Norfolk and Portsmouth yards underwent tremendous improvements from 1840 to 1860. A new building slip began at Norfolk in 1845. In August 1846, the lot on the North side of the Navy yard, known as Saint Helena, was purchased and added to the yard. Almost immediately storehouses, a blacksmith shop with a turning machine, a foundry, and a plumbing shop began to be assembled to increase advancements at the yard and make it competitive with private yards. In 1848, workers completed the quay wall and began building the new cofferdam. In addition, magazines slowly appeared on the newly acquired Fort Norfolk land transferred from the War Department to the Navy.

At Portsmouth, a boathouse and landing were built in 1844 and the powder magazine completed construction in 1849. In 1851, the yard extended the shiphouse to maintain the newer longer Navy ships. Also added were a cooper's shop, watchman's quarters, ordnance house, administrative offices, and a muster room. All of these improvements to the main navy yards showed a cohesive effort by the Navy Department and Congress to create self-sufficient, forward-looking installations that could eventually compete with the main naval powers of the day.

Security at naval facilities became a top issue in the late nineteenth century. While each installation was properly enclosed, the walls could be easily scaled in the dark of night. One solution to this security dilemma was properly lighting the yards. Originally, lanterns lit the yards; however, the Navy installed gas fixtures for the first time at Boston in 1853 and Norfolk in 1855. Nonetheless, as late as 1880, lanterns were still the main source of lighting at most naval facilities. That year Key West Naval Station requested "three street lanterns" to more thoroughly light the naval grounds.

Although Congress had appropriated additional funds for the ironclads during the 1880s, Secretary of the Navy William Chandler significantly reduced the budget spent maintaining and staffing the navy yards. In 1883 he closed the Pensacola, Philadelphia, and New London yards, discontinued the construction and repair of ships in Boston, and reduced the size of the Portsmouth yard. This policy of neglect remained in effect until the Spanish-American War, and was one of the major reasons why the Navy was ill prepared for war.

Throughout this time, the Navy approved very limited appropriations for the care and maintenance of installations, which resulted in decaying buildings, docks, and wharves. In 1890, the naval shore establishment consisted of thirteen navy yards and stations covering 2605 acres, with 439 workshops, stores, and shiphouses; 7.18 miles of wharf line; 10 dry docks; 19 marine railways and launching ways; 150 horses and oxen; and 96 houses for officers' quarters. The Bureau of Yards and Docks routinely requested a yearly budget increase

Workers rebuild railroad tracks on First Street at the New York Navy Yard, 1919. During World War I, many of the yards had new standard-gauge track laid to serve the industrial shops and provide ease of access to the waterfront. Simultaneously, new streets were installed of vitrified brick, wood block, or concrete for the new vehicles with rubber tires. *Courtesy of the U.S. Navy Seabee Museum.*

to $800,000 a year to maintain the necessary improvements at the navy yards. Congress and the Navy continued, however, to appropriate only $62,500 a year for maintenance of the vast naval facilities, which caused the disrepair and deterioration of the shore establishment.

In 1897, all public works in the then existing thirteen navy yards and naval stations were valued at $53 million dollars. The dry docks and buildings were small, old, and more suited to the repair of 1860-era ships than the White Squadron of the 1880s. The buildings were inadequately heated and lighted, they were almost devoid of cranes, and the power facilities were insufficient. The naval waterfronts also afforded insufficient space for vessel repairing, outfitting, or the discharging of stores. Secretary of the Navy John Davis Long organized the Bunce Board to discover the inadequacies of the dry docks and create a plan to expand and repair them. The Navy ignored the board's recommendations until after the Spanish-American War began.

The Navy eventually acknowledged its inadequacies and launched steps to create modern shops, improved waterfronts, build superior dry docks, and construct advanced coaling facilities. Four timber graving docks were authorized by Congress to be built at Portsmouth, Boston, Philadelphia, and Mare Island on May 4, 1898. Facilities expanded and construction budgets flowed for several years following the war, which greatly assisted the long neglected and overlooked yards and stations. However, these desperately needed funds did not last long.

Another area of public works was the installation of electrical plants at navy yards. In 1890, the Bureau of Yards and Docks installed the first electric plant at the Washington Navy Yard to light all streets

Granite from an old sea wall piled near the Joiner's Shop, Building 36, at the Boston Navy Yard, May 15, 1899. The granite from the sea wall was later reused in the construction of Dry Dock Number 2. *Courtesy of the U.S. Navy Seabee Museum.*

and gun shops. By 1900, the yards at Mare Island, Boston, New York, Port Royal, Norfolk, and Pensacola all had electrical plants. The efforts to provide modern shops and mechanized equipment on the waterfront areas, as well as extensive dry docks and improved coaling facilities, resulted in a large number of power plants at the yards. It soon became apparent that there was significant duplication in generating equipment and distribution systems due to each Bureau building and maintaining its own power sources. The Naval Act of 1904 provided for centralizing all power plants and distribution systems at the facilities under the cognizance of the Bureau of Yards and Docks. In accordance with this law, the Bureau of Yards and Docks established a central power plant serving all activities at each Navy yard and naval station.

The savings earned from centralizing power at each naval installation persuaded Congress and the Navy Department to look for further savings in other areas. One area suggested was the consolidation of the naval construction projects. At this time, each Bureau designed and erected its own facilities. By placing the construction function under the civil engineers of the Bureau of Yards and Docks the Navy could avoid duplication, consolidate resources, and best utilize labor. On January 28, 1911, the House Naval Affairs Committee instigated a change to facilitate better work coordination in the matter of naval construction. The passage of the naval appropriations act of April 4, 1911, charged the Bureau of Yards and Docks with the design and construction of the public works and public utilities of the Navy, irrespective of the Bureau or office of the Navy

Department that may use or operate them and the appropriation or fund from which their costs were defrayed. This consolidation greatly streamlined expenses and organized the Navy's real property assets.

In 1913, Navy public works were valued at $191 million dollars. While naval public works had expanded since the beginning of the Spanish-American War, its growth was not commensurate with that of the fleet. After the beginning of World War I in 1914, the Navy completed a thorough survey of its resources and it became obvious that if the country were drawn into war it would be necessary to make immense additions to the fleet, the naval shore facilities, and to the merchant marine.

The Shore Station Development Board, established in 1916, served the dual purpose of coordinating the various Bureau public works programs and making general long-range plans to guide the development of the shore establishment. With expenditures for public works held to a minimum, the tendency was to consider only needs that were immediate and urgent. However, the prospect of obtaining the necessary approval and funding for future planning remained remote.

On May 2, 1916, the Secretary of the Navy appointed the Board for the Development of Navy Yard Plans to draw up comprehensive development plans for each base and the essential features for each individual base to meet all their needs. In order to avoid numerous meetings of the whole board,

Personnel in the drafting room at the Public Works Department, Puget Sound Naval Shipyard, 1936. Under the first Deficiency Act of 1931, the Bureau began a construction program of public works which not only provided a new and much-needed field of employment, but also gave the shore establishment vital improvements. *Courtesy of the U.S. Navy Seabee Museum.*

One of the workmen outside the Mare Island Navy Yard stables at Building 88 bringing in a load of wood to heat Quarters A, December 1860. *Courtesy of the National Archives.*

View of the Cumberland Street entrance at the New York Navy Yard and its new gate, March 30, 1937. The gate was formerly in line with the fence and was remodeled with WPA Project funds. Except during specific hours when Marine Corps guards were on duty to permit traffic and pedestrian access, the gate was kept closed. *Courtesy of the U.S. Navy Seabee Museum.*

Trolley tracks outside the construction machine shop, Building 115, at the New York Navy Yard, January 2, 1914. The machine shop was a large building with two main center aisles for heavy machinery and erection work with two 15-ton cranes. *Courtesy of the U.S. Navy Seabee Museum.*

a sub-board consisting of representatives from the Bureaus of Yards and Docks, Steam Engineering, and Construction and Repair met to develop sketches, plans, estimates, and lists of all requirements for presentation to the whole board. The sub-board first developed the "type plans" for each type of base. This included each of the bases and facilities necessary for a navy yard, hospital complex, ordnance facility, naval station, etc. Once the purported ideal plan of development was completed and approved by the entire board, construction at each base quickly began.

Once the U.S. declared war, the Navy underwent phenomenal growth in war materiel and personnel from 1917 to 1918. Until the United States entered World War I, naval public works were confined to the continental states and its territories. During the war, the United States constructed public works in France and Britain to support the fleet and aid its allies in the tenuous years afterward.

The Bureau of Yards and Docks accomplished an enormous amount of construction during World War I, including building training facilities, hospital facilities, shipyard development, dry docks, power plants, ordnance depots, and storage facilities. A major development during this period was the establishment of air stations and submarine bases, which required a new set of construction requirements. The Bureau let contracts for the construction of dirigible hangars, steel-framed seaplane hangars, shops, storehouses, powerhouses, and quarters at most of the new air patrol stations along the Atlantic coast. Another new construction issue revolved around the fleet transitioning to oil to propel naval vessels, which required the construction of Petroleum-Oil-Lubricant (POL) storage facilities to stockpile the fuel.

Fuel oil tank #39-A, erected at the Charleston Navy Yard, South Carolina, March 28, 1913. The gradual reduction in the supply of petroleum fuel from wells in the United States led the Navy to construct large petroleum storage facilities at various points along the East coast so that the fuel could be held in reserve in case of emergency or war. *Courtesy of the U.S. Navy Seabee Museum.*

Civil Works Appropriation (CWA) Project Number 3 included clearing and dressing the railroad embankment at the north end of the Charleston Navy Yard, view looking north, April 20, 1934. As part of the WPA program, the Bureau of Yards and Docks began public works construction projects to rebuild the navy yards and bring vital improvements to the shore establishment and employment to the country.
Courtesy of the U.S. Navy Seabee Museum.

Workers inspect a row of 22" pipe before they are installed as part of the new water supply system at the Yerba Buena Island Naval Station, San Francisco, California, November 12, 1937. The project was part of the Works Progress Administration (WPA) and overseen by the Bureau of Yards and Docks. *Courtesy of the National Archives.*

Commandant's House on Chelsea Street at the Boston Navy Yard, Massachusetts, October 1934. Arthur C. Haskell, Photographer. *Courtesy of Library of Congress, Historic American Buildings Survey Collection.*

The total expenditures for all public works carried out under the supervision of the Bureau of Yards and Docks during the war years were more than the total expenditure that had been made at all navy yards and naval stations during the preceding 116 years. The overall Navy real estate and public works value more than doubled from about $211 million to $469 million.

The general development work carried on at navy yards and stations continued throughout the interwar years. Engineers and workers made improvements and extensions to streets, tracks, and sewers in connection with shipbuilding development. One construction project included expanding base railroad systems, as well as adding hammerhead cranes, the erection of gantries, and standing gauge equipment at several sites adjacent to the dry docks to assist in loading and repair work. At Puget Sound, in addition to the routine waterfront work of maintaining dikes and dredging at the yards, damage done by the invasion of marine borers into the waters necessitated reconstruction work at the timber wharves, quay walls, moorings, dikes, and causeways.

Despite the strict control on naval expansion, several major projects were undertaken in the period between the wars. In 1920, the Navy established a Naval Experimental and Research Laboratory to provide a central location for all naval research and development. The physical complex, four miles south of the Washington Navy Yard, included a three-story laboratory and office building, machine shop, foundry and forge shop, a pattern and storage building, and a power plant. The Naval Experimental and Research Laboratory undertook new research into gun erosion, torpedo motive power, and the improvement of submarine engines.

Additional construction projects included a long breakwater and nine finger piers at the newly designated submarine base at Key West, Florida, in 1920. In Astoria, Oregon, a submarine and destroyer base included the construction of bulkheads, piers, the dredging of basin and channel, and the filling of areas behind bulkheads.

Inspection District and Power Section staff pose for a photograph at the Puget Sound Naval Shipyard, 1936. The Inspection District was charged with inspecting all engineering materials that required special tests or examination at the point of or during the process of manufacturing. *Courtesy of the U.S. Navy Seabee Museum.*

The naval complex in San Diego was another major construction effort undertaken by the Navy. The extensive San Diego naval facilities included a large fuel oil depot with a 4.2 million gallon capacity, repair and supply facilities for the fleet, a model training station to accommodate 4,500 officers and enlisted men, and an immense fleet supply storehouse.

Between the World Wars, the shore establishment witnessed the addition of numerous dry docks and marine railways. Naval engineers constructed docking facilities at Boston, Philadelphia, Norfolk, Charleston, Pearl Harbor, Hunter's Point, and Puget Sound. The Navy, trying to bring the aging navy yards into the twentieth century, installed new power sources at most naval bases, including the first automatic motor generating station built at the Puget Sound Navy Yard in 1928. They also added telephone systems and elevators to some buildings.

The Navy repeatedly reminded Congress that the shore establishment lacked behind the fleet. They warned that this could dangerously impair the forces afloat if the Navy failed to procure additional funds to increase scientific industrialization and base

Loading a Coal Lighter at Building 109, Boston Navy Yard, Massachusetts, November 23, 1912. Navy colliers were bulk cargo ships designed to carry coal, especially for use by coal-fired warships. In the late nineteenth century, numerous wooden-hulled sailing colliers were adapted for use in extensive voyages to the South Pacific. *Courtesy of the U.S. Navy Seabee Museum.*

facilities. The condition of the naval shore establishment reached a low ebb in 1930. The reduction in the Armed Services following World War I found the Bureau of Yards and Docks with only 113 permanent Civil Engineer Corps officers scattered throughout the entire shore establishment, assisted by approximately 500 civilian employees.

During the early thirties, the Defense Establishment operated at an extremely low level of efficiency. The Great Depression and the increasing threat from Germany in the latter part of the 1930s greatly affected the Bureau and its work. Under the First Deficiency Act of 1931, the Bureau began a construction program of public works that not only provided a new and much-needed field of employment, but also gave the shore establishment vital improvements. As part of the Works Progress Administration, the Bureau administered all funds allotted to the Navy and allocated them to various construction projects.

View of Radio Tower Number 1 from the southeast at the U.S. Naval Hospital, Chelsea, Massachusetts, August 22, 1921. Until the development of high-frequency radio transmissions, the more powerful naval radio stations required high towers capable of resisting large antennae pulls, as well as the effects of high winds. Radio tower designs were standardized from heights of 100 feet to 600 feet. The highest self-supporting towers built by the Navy were those at the great station at Croix d'Hins, near Bordeaux, France, built immediately after World War I. The eight towers were each 820 feet high and built to maintain communications with our expeditionary forces in case all telegraph cables to Europe were cut by enemy submarines. *Courtesy of the U.S. Navy Seabee Museum.*

Interior of the Fire Station at Mare Island Navy Yard showing period Fire Engine, August 15, 1919. The Mare Island Fire Station was constructed in 1900 on the northeast corner of California Avenue and Central Street. In 1916, the fire station moved to allow the extension of the shipbuilding ways. This structure was the first steel frame construction at the shipyard built after the 1898 earthquake. *Courtesy of Library of Congress, Historic American Buildings Survey Collection.*

In response to the growing unrest in Europe during the late 1930s, the United States began developing military equipment, workers, and infrastructure plans to prepare for the Axis threat. Congress, through the Second Vinson Act of 1938, authorized the first significant naval expansion after World War I, which called for a 20 percent increase in ships and an increase in aircraft strength to 3,000 planes. The law also directed the Secretary of the Navy to appoint a board to determine the additional shore facilities required to support the enlarged fleet.

In 1934, with the passage of the Vinson-Trammell Act, Congress reestablished the Shore Station Development Board to build up the fleet to the limits agreed upon by the Washington and London treaties. In view of the newly authorized increase in strength, the Navy established a list of priorities for future construction. The West Coast, Canal Zone, the Hawaiian Islands, the Philippines, and Guam received the highest "A" classification. The bases at New York, Boston, Philadelphia, and Chesapeake received a "B" classification; Key West, Charleston, Pensacola, and Guantanamo Bay a "C"; and a "D" to Great Lakes, Alaska, and Samoa. These classifications were not strictly adhered to, but were used as a guideline and pattern for the work of the Board.

Prior to December 1941, the Navy's public works planning revolved around building the shore establishment to meet the needs of the Two-Ocean Navy recently approved by Congress. This planning followed the recommendations of the Hepburn Board and the Greenslade Board. There were two types of emergency facilities provided for in the recommendations. One included the specification of additional facilities, including shipbuilding, aircraft construction facilities, and training facilities for large numbers of recruits. In developing the emergency facilities for the bases, each Bureau, Office of Naval Operations, Naval District Commandant, or Commander designed the requirements for fulfilling the mission assigned to it by the Chief of Naval Operations.

Base public works crew rebuilding railroad tracks on Perry Avenue at the New York Navy Yard looking southeast, October 5, 1914. Railroad tracks for handling ship materials and freight were common at all navy yards by 1865. In 1862, the Bureau of Yards and Docks proposed to lay tracks from the storehouses and principal workshops to the wharves to expedite transportation of stores and heavy articles. Rail tracks cut down on the cost of transporting heavy articles around the yard. Rail transportation systems were installed as early as 1844 at the Pensacola Navy Yard to transport supplies and ease construction at the yard. Since the majority of naval facilities were situated on the waterfront, most supplies were transported by ship or hauled overland by draft animals. However, shipping overland was slow, expensive, and subject to weather issues. Beginning in 1857, tracks were laid at naval facilities to connect the station with the commercial railroads that were beginning to stretch across the nation. *Courtesy of the U.S. Navy Seabee Museum.*

View of Construction and Repair Workshops, Buildings 51 and 56, at the Mare Island Navy Yard showing skylights on the roofs for blueprint processing and lighting, 1915. *Courtesy of Library of Congress, Historic American Engineering Record Collection.*

The year and a half prior to the attack on Pearl Harbor had been a time of rapid transition from a peacetime to a war economy, and the Navy's public works program had to align itself with the country's wartime plan. The Bureau of Yards and Docks and the Civil Engineer Corps not only oversaw continental construction of 10 supply depots; 50 fuel, landing craft equipment, and aviation depots; 4 major shipping facilities; 5 coastal ammunition depots; and 42 new hospitals, but also commanded the Seabees, who constructed more than 400 bases worldwide in every combat theater during World War II. Part of the Navy's successful construction expansion during World War II can be directly linked to the 140 previous years of public works construction, management, and growth. This sound structure increased the Navy's ability to react and effect change quickly in the face of impending war on two fronts.

Civilian and Naval personnel working at the Main Navy or Munitions Buildings, Navy Department, Washington, D.C., c. 1918. This office was on an upper floor at the south end of one of the buildings' wings. *Courtesy of the Naval History and Heritage Command.*

Laying tracks to the structural shop on Morris Avenue looking South from 2nd Street, New York Navy Yard, September 1, 1919. During World War I, the Bureau redesigned the New York Navy Yard foundry, smithery, and machine shop into an all-in-one structural shop. The shop was designed to handle raw material from steel storage at one end through smelting, casting, fabrication, and final erection at the other end. *Courtesy of the U.S. Navy Seabee Museum.*

Several U.S. Marines guard the first electric motor driven pay wagon in use on payday at the Washington Navy Yard, c. 1917-1918. *Courtesy of the Naval History and Heritage Command.*

Radio Arlington as it looked when commissioned in 1913. As early as 1899, the Navy became interested in employing radio as a means of rapid communication between the fleet and the shore establishment. Early naval radio stations used small antennae supported from wood-guyed masts at a low height. With increasing demands for distance, more powerful equipment and larger antennae became necessary. Radio Arlington, completed February 13, 1913, became the first high power station, with one 600-foot and two 450-foot steel self-supporting towers erected to support the antennae. *Courtesy of the U.S. Navy Seabee Museum*

Early on, the Navy was interested in employing radio as a means of rapid communication between the fleet and the shore establishment. They had been experimenting with wireless telegraphy since 1899, when the first official U.S. Navy telegraph message was sent from the steamship USS *Conce* to the Navy's Highland Station on the Jersey Coast. By 1904, 18 naval shore stations and 33 naval ships were radio equipped. By 1908, one-half of the 387 wireless stations in the world were manned by United States naval personnel.

On February 13, 1913, its first high-powered radio station, Radio Arlington, was commissioned. This was also the first time a wireless station was called a radio station. From 1914 to 1915, the construction of medium power stations progressed extensively. Foundations and self-supporting towers, ranging from 250 to 300 feet in height, were built at the Boston Navy Yard; Key West, Florida; Guantanamo Bay, Cuba; Great Lakes, Michigan; San Juan, Puerto Rico; and Cordova, Alaska. These stations were equipped with operating buildings, quarters, barracks, wharves, and storehouses.

During World War I, the number and capacity of transmitters at naval radio stations increased. The Navy built towers, buildings, and other facilities, in addition to the construction of several 600-foot high radio towers at Cavite, Pearl Harbor, and San Diego. Similar stations were built at Cayey, Puerto Rico, in 1917, and at Greenbury Point, Annapolis, Maryland, in 1918. In 1919, the Navy was instrumental in helping to create the Radio Corporation of America. It began scheduled broadcasts in 1920 from Naval Support Facility Anacostia, making it the first radio broadcast in the District of Columbia.

Coal wharf at the Puget Sound Naval Shipyard, Washington, March 20, 1923. The Navy required the best grade of bituminous coal for steam purposes. After years of elaborate chemical and practical tests, the Navy compiled standard specifications for coal used by Navy ships. For many years after steam propelled engines were installed on naval ships, most cruising was still undertaken by sail and steam was minimally used. Each of the major naval facilities had a few coal sheds without mechanical equipment that had been provided for storing the small amount of coal the Navy carried in stock. *Courtesy of the National Archives.*

Worker at the U.S. Naval Station Olongapo coaling plant uses an auxiliary method to load coal using buckets and a rail system, September 2, 1913. *Courtesy of the U.S. Navy Seabee Museum.*

In June 1816, a catamaran steam frigate, the *Fulton*, became the first steam powered paddle-wheel warship and the first Navy ship to use steam as a source of propulsion. Due to the efforts of visionary men like Commodore Matthew Perry, a vocal proponent of modernizing the Navy, the Navy became interested in building steam powered naval ships.

The new steam powered fleet led to the establishment of the naval coaling station. By 1855, the increase in steam for ship propulsion raised the question of establishing coaling stations both at home and at select international locations. By 1857, funds were appropriated for establishing a coal depot at Key West, Florida, and another at Port Royal, South Carolina, in 1886.

The Navy's transition to steam powered vessels also required overseas fueling bases at strategic locations. The expansion of European colonies in the Pacific made the search for suitable locations for U.S. facilities difficult. Permanent coaling stations did not appear on foreign soil until 1878, when steps were taken to establish one at Pago Pago, Samoa. In the early 1860s a temporary coaling station had

USS *New Hampshire* (Battleship #25) taking on coal from a barge moored alongside her at the New York Navy Yard, c. 1909. The breakout of war with Spain made the need for coaling facilities come to the forefront of naval issues. The Navy discovered that not one yard in the U.S. had the proper provisions for storing a large supply of coal or the modern machinery for loading it on board ships. The war demonstrated to the Navy the necessity to have on hand sufficient fuel to make it independent of the lapses and shortcomings in private source coal supply. Commander Bradford, Chief of the Bureau of Equipment, also demanded modern devices for coaling battleships quickly. As a result, the Belknap Board recommended the establishment of modern coaling stations equipped with mechanized equipment. *Courtesy of the Naval History and Heritage Command and John B. Dowty, 12th Naval District Museum.*

been established in Hawaii, but was abandoned a short time later. At that time, the Navy was still leaning heavily on sail power and had little use for permanent coaling stations. In 1872, the U.S. surveyed Pearl Harbor for use as a possible naval station. In 1884, after a series of negotiations with King Kalakaua of Hawaii, the United States was granted exclusive rights to enter the harbor and establish a coaling and repair station. This included the right to improve the entrance to the harbor and construct all needed facilities for an operational coaling station.

For many years after steam propelled engines were installed in naval ships, most cruising was still undertaken by sail and steam was minimally used. Each of the major naval facilities had a few coal sheds without mechanical equipment for storing the small amount of coal the Navy carried in stock. Shortly after the outbreak of the Spanish-American War, the Belknap Board made a study of the coaling stations and discovered that not one Navy yard in the nation had the proper provisions for storing large supplies of coal or the modern machinery for loading it on board ships. The board recommended the establishment

Public Works Department dredges Agana Harbor in Guam, c. 1924. As part of this project, the Navy began dredging operations to deepen the channel across the reef, from the inner harbor to Piti, and the channel to Suamy to allow ships to enter the harbor at low tide. *Courtesy of the U.S. Navy Seabee Museum.*

of modern coaling stations equipped with mechanized equipment. The initial stations were built at Frenchman's Bay, Maine; Portsmouth, Maine; Boston, Massachusetts; New London, Connecticut; New York, New York; Philadelphia, Pennsylvania; Washington, D.C.; Norfolk, Virginia; and Port Royal, South Carolina. The Navy eventually built proper coaling facilities at all the main yards and stations along both coasts.

At the turn of the nineteenth century, the Navy thought liquid fuel was only a helpful auxiliary to coal. In 1904, the annual consumption of coal for Navy ships was 350,000 tons. The Navy used a higher quality of bituminous coal than was available at most foreign ports, thus necessitating coal storage at specified locations around the world. The treaty following the war with Spain gave the U.S. possession rights, which led to the establishment of naval stations and coaling stations at various strategic overseas locations in the Philippines, Guam, Cuba, and Puerto Rico.

One of the concerns facing the Navy with oversees coaling stations was the need to heavily fortify the facilities, or they would simply serve as a supply source for U.S. adversaries. Each station had to be capable of defending itself without the aid of the fleet, and the men stationed there trained to destroy the storage plant when seriously threatened. The Navy had neither the inclination nor the funding to properly fortify numerous international facilities, leaving only a few stations around the world to supply the fleet with high grade bituminous coal.

During the winter of 1917-1918, the shortage of coal on the east coast was so acute it motivated the Navy to establish emergency storage depots for coal at principle ports. These new stations were equipped with modern cableway trestles, locomotive cranes with clamshell buckets, locomotives, and side-dump railroad cars to transport the coal from the depot to the coal dumper.

Early in the twentieth century, the Navy determined that liquid fuel exclusively would power its new generation of fighting ships. In September 1909, Secretary of the Interior Richard A. Ballinger suggested to President Taft that the petroleum and oil shale reserves be maintained for the exclusive use of the Navy in case of a national emergency. The Navy originally envisioned it as a reserve supply of crude oil to fuel U.S. naval vessels in times of short supply or emergencies. After a series of Executive Orders passed, Presidents Taft and Wilson permanently set aside three naval petroleum

Railroad track repairs at the causeway entrance looking north at the New York Navy Yard, April 30, 1915.
Courtesy of the U.S. Navy Seabee Museum.

reserves at Elk Hills, California; Buena Vista, California; and Teapot Dome, Wyoming. Altogether, the reserves encompassed about fifty thousand acres of public land. The fourth Naval Petroleum Reserve in Point Barrow, Alaska, was set aside in 1923, although the petroleum opportunities were only superficially explored until World War II, when it became essential to investigate the area fully.

Three Naval Oil-Shale Reserves were also set aside from public lands for the exclusive use and benefit of the Navy. To provide a secondary possible source of fuel, portions of the vast oil shale-bearing formation in Colorado and Utah were set aside by Executive Order on December 6, 1916. Legislation permitting the Navy to take possession of the reserves, drilling wells, erect refineries, and produce its own supply of fuel was not given until 1920.

With the change in naval vessels from coal to oil fuel, the importance of coaling plants decreased. The transition from coal to oil as a major propellant required the construction of new fuel facilities, including tanks, pipelines, and pumping plants. These new depots consisted of a grouping of reinforced concrete storage tanks set underground and equipped with heating coils and a fire protection system. During World War I, the need for steel in the shipbuilding industry caused the Bureau to abandon its use of steel storage tanks for fuel oil and instead build underground concrete reservoirs. After the war, the standard returned to steel tanks for oil storage. The Navy's first oil storage facility, built at Guantanamo Bay, Cuba, had a capacity for 6 million gallons of oil. The Navy constructed a subsequent station at Yorktown, Virginia, that could hold 30 million gallons.

View of the Old Navy Department Building at 17th Street between "F" and "G" Streets, c. 1870.
Courtesy of the Naval History and Heritage Command.

Authorized by the act of Congress approved March 3, 1871, the State, War, and Navy Building was built between 1871 and 1888 in the French Second Empire style. The Old Executive Office Building south wing was begun in 1871. In July 1872, while the south wing was still in progress, ground was broken for the east wing.

The entire east wing was completed for occupancy April 16, 1879, whereupon the Navy and War Departments at once moved into the building. The Navy occupied the southern half and the War the northern half, pending the construction of the northern wing.

The west and center wings were simultaneously erected, and covered the site of the Old Navy Building on 17th St. between "G" and "F" streets. The demolition of this old building commenced February 18, 1884, and finished March 31, 1884. The wings built on this site were completed for occupancy January 1886. Early in February 1886, the several Bureaus of the War Department began moving into these wings.

Designed by Alfred B. Mullett, Supervising Architect, the building has 552 rooms and 2 miles of black and white tiled corridors. Richard

The State, War, and Navy Building, also known as the Old Executive Office Building or Eisenhower Executive Office Building, located at Pennsylvania Avenue and 17th Street, NW, in Washington, D.C., c. 1917. The building, an example of French Second Empire architecture, was constructed in 1871 and designed by Alfred B. Mullett. It was designated a National Historic Landmark in 1969. *Courtesy of the Library of Congress.*

von Ezdorf designed the interior, with the detail made almost entirely of cast iron or plaster. The use of wood was minimized to insure fire safety. Eight massive granite staircases with over 4,000 individually cast bronze balusters are capped by four skylight domes and two stained glass rotundas. Decorative elements included doorknobs with cast patterns indicating which of the original three occupying departments (State, Navy, or War) occupied a particular space.

Gradually, the original tenants of the building vacated: the Navy Department in 1918 (except for the Secretary, who stayed until 1921), followed by the War Department in 1938, and finally by the State Department in 1947. The White House commenced moving some of its offices into the building in 1939, and in 1949, the Executive Office of the President assumed responsibility and renamed it the Executive Office Building. The building now houses various agencies that comprise the Executive Office of the President, such as the White House Office, the Office of the Vice President, the Office of Management and Budget, and the National Security Council.

The monumental State, War, and Navy Building adjacent to the White House became inadequate to house the departments long before World War I, which forced various Bureaus of the War and the Navy Departments to seek office space elsewhere. Three years before the war, the Navy rented a nine-story building near the corner of Eighteenth Street and New York Avenue.

The threat of war caused further overrunning of office space, and the declaration of war produced unprecedented numbers of civilians and military personnel to overtake Washington, D.C. By July 1, 1917, the Navy Department occupied nine different buildings and severely overcrowded all of them.

The War Department formulated an idea to house the entire overflow of the Navy Department and all homeless agencies of the War Department in an enormous block of temporary three story frame and pebbledash buildings at Sixth and B Streets, between the Lincoln and Washington Memorials. Once completed, a 100-foot covered bridge connected the Navy and Munitions Buildings.

The maximum construction force of the buildings, including both skilled and unskilled labor in the employ of general contractor and all subcontractors, was approximately 3,400 men. Because of the volume of labor, high morale, and patriotic spirit of the employees, the building was completed in 5 ½ months.

Tremie staging area and tower at the New York Navy Yard shipbuilding ways, June 10, 1929. A tremie is an apparatus for depositing and consolidating concrete under water. *Courtesy of the U.S. Navy Seabee Museum.*

View of the Washington Navy Yard looking south down Dahlgren Avenue from atop the Main Entrance (Latrobe Gate), c. 1900. The large structure to the right is the North Gun Shop, Buildings 40 and 41, with the South Gun Shop and Breech Mechanism Shop, Building 76, beyond it. The Commandant's Office, Building 1, is at the foot of Dahlgren Avenue. Leutze Park is at left, with Building 57, the Ordnance School, at its southern end. *Courtesy of the Naval History and Heritage Command and Lawrence Gichner.*

Photograph of the railroad connections over the Dry Dock Number 4 caisson, east end looking northwest, New York Navy Yard, September 4, 1913.
Courtesy of the U.S. Navy Seabee Museum.

Coaling plant at the Puget Sound Naval Shipyard, Washington, view looking north, April 1, 1913. Shortly after the outbreak of the Spanish-American War, a study of the coaling stations revealed that not one navy yard in the nation had the proper provisions for storing large supplies of coal or the modern machinery for loading it on board ships. Modern coaling stations equipped with mechanized equipment were eventually built at all the main navy yards and stations along both coasts. *Courtesy of the U.S. Navy Seabee Museum.*

The Central Power Station at Puget Naval Shipyard was constructed in 1910 as the shipyard's first central steam power station. The Central Power Station was the principal power plant for the buildings and equipment at the industrial yard. Until the construction of the West End Boiler Plant in 1918 it was the sole power plant at the yard, and was therefore an important facility in the early operations of the shipyard. *Courtesy of the U.S. Navy Seabee Museum.*

Coaling plant powerhouse at the U.S. Naval Coaling Station, Olongapo, Philippines, September 1, 1908. In 1904, the United States established a coaling station at Olongapo after the treaty with Spain gave the U.S. rights to establish overseas bases. In 1904, the annual consumption of coal for navy ships was 350,000 tons. The Navy used a higher quality of bituminous coal than was available at most foreign ports, thus necessitating coal storage at key locations around the world. *Courtesy of the U.S. Navy Seabee Museum.*

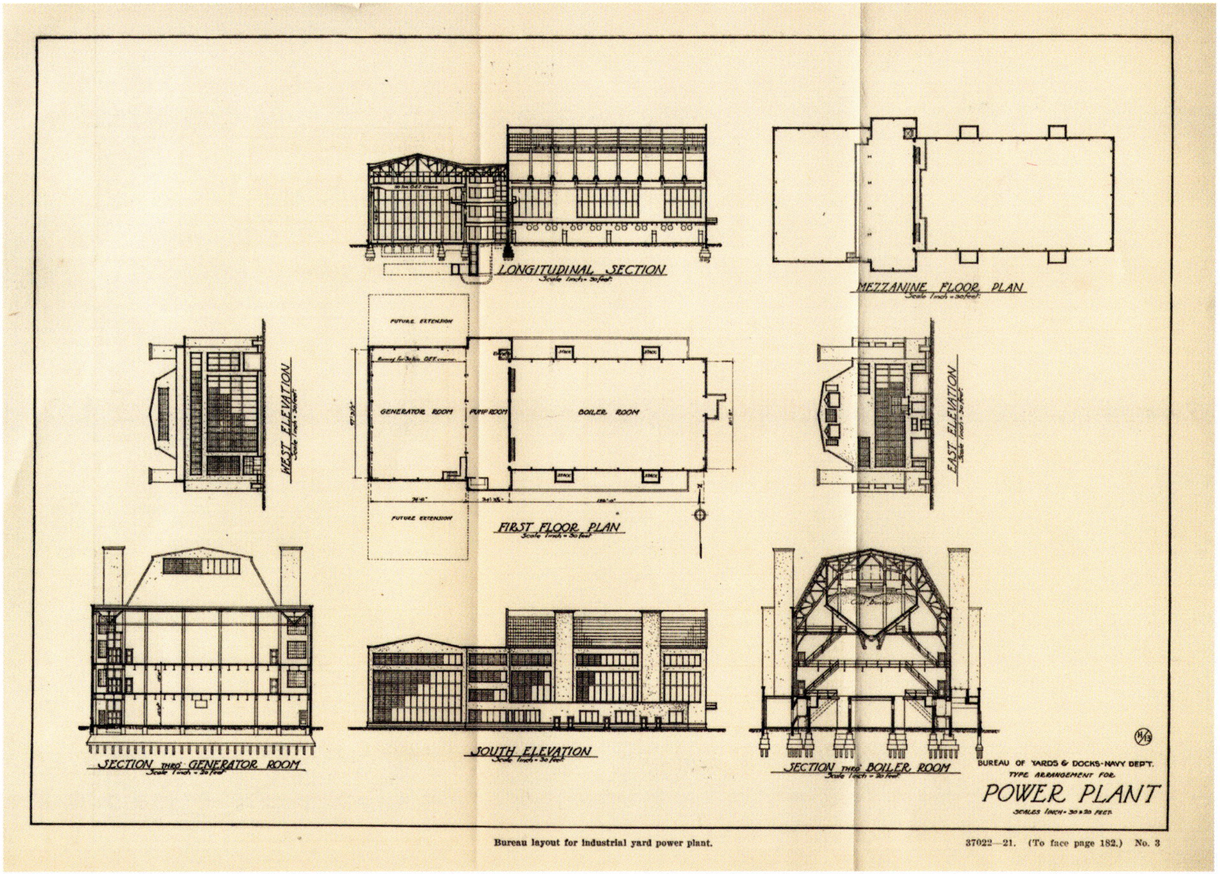

Design drawing of a typical naval station power plant designed by the Bureau of Yards and Docks in 1918. The Bureau of Yards and Docks drew up standardized plans to design new power plants in accordance with modern practice containing high efficiency power generated apparatus and with space for future expansion. *Courtesy of the U.S. Navy Seabee Museum.*

Chute runway and coal hoist foundation at the coaling plant, Building 129, New York Navy Yard, looking northwest, July 23, 1919. The design and specifications for the coaling facilities at the New York Navy Yard included a building with a storage capacity of 10,000 tons with its general dimensions being 290 feet in length, 97 feet wide, and a height of 35 feet. The building was located near the water's edge with new mechanisms to unload the coal from the railway and easily load the ships. *Courtesy of the U.S. Navy Seabee Museum.*

Workers raise the last truss into position over two industrial shops at the New York Navy Yard, January 13, 1936. This project consolidated the Blacksmith and Forge Shop, Building 11, and the Pipe and Copper Shop, Building 12. It was one of the many Works Progress Administration (WPA) projects administered by the Navy to get the country back to work. *Courtesy of the U.S. Navy Seabee Museum.*

The Bureau of Yards and Docks oversaw the consolidation of two industrial shops as part of the Works Progress Administration at the New York Navy Yard, January 12, 1936. Workers are completing roof trusses and sheathing. *Courtesy of the U.S. Navy Seabee Museum.*

SANGLEY POINT.
COALING STATION.
NAVAL MAGAZINE.

Photograph of the U.S. Naval Station Cavite, Philippines, waterfront, 1905. LT(jg) Archibald Parsons, later Rear Admiral and Chief of the Bureau of Yards and Docks, captured this and numerous other images of the Cavite station while he served as Public Works Officer from 1904 to 1906. The first Civil Engineer Corps officer arrived at Cavite in 1901 to design and build the base infrastructure with no staff, office, workshops, or budget. *Courtesy of the U.S. Navy Seabee Museum.*

The Public Works Department and main offices in Agana, Guam, c. 1924 (l to r): view of the Disbursing Office, Governor's Palace, Public Works Office, Marine Barracks, and old bandstand in the Plaza de España, which has been the center stage in Agana for many government and civic activities since the Spanish landed in 1669. In 1944, the Governor's Palace was destroyed during the liberation of Guam. *Courtesy of the U.S. Navy Seabee Museum.*

Radio Tower at New London Naval Submarine Base, Connecticut, June 2, 1928. All naval radio stations were operated by and all new radio projects initiated with the Bureau of Engineering. The design and construction of all public works related to radio stations, as well as any additions to the facilities of existing stations were handled by the Bureau of Yards and Docks which, when requested to do so, designed and constructed many new stations. *Courtesy of the U.S. Navy Seabee Museum.*

Transportation crew stands outside the main shop at the Puget Sound Naval Shipyard, 1936. The transportation division, which included the operation and management of motor vehicles, locomotives, and trucks, remained one of the busiest branches of the Public Works Department. Vehicles all operated out of a central organization to maintain control of all the base vehicles. The Navy centralized the department into one large shop to see to the repair and rebuilding of all base vehicles. *Courtesy of the U.S. Navy Seabee Museum.*

Workers install the main pipe system for the Naval Research Laboratory, District of Columbia, 1919. In 1916, Congress allocated $1.5 million towards building this great research laboratory, but it was not completed until after World War I. The Naval Research Laboratory began operations in 1923 as the Navy's first modern scientific research institution, and it continues today as one of the Navy's leading research and development laboratories. *Courtesy of the U.S. Navy Seabee Museum.*

View of the Pearl Harbor Coaling Station's rail system, 1919. An 1887 treaty between the U.S. and King Kalakaua granted the United States exclusive rights to Pearl Harbor and permission to construct a coaling station and repair facility inside the harbor. In May 1899, the Navy established a 1000-ton coaling station in downtown Pearl Harbor with plans to increase that capacity 20-fold. *Courtesy of the U.S. Navy Seabee Museum.*

The Hawaiian Dredging Company dredges Dry Dock No. 3 at the Pearl Harbor Navy Yard, 1940. On December 22, 1939, the Navy awarded an additional contract as part of the Hepburn Report for the construction of two additional graving docks adjacent to the existing battleship dry dock in Pearl Harbor. The Bureau of Yards and Docks designed Dry Dock No. 2 to accommodate a 1,000-foot battleship, while Dry Dock No. 3, at 497 feet, was designed for destroyers and submarines. *Courtesy of the U.S. Navy Seabee Museum.*

Workers begin excavation for the Structural Shop foundation at the New York Navy Yard, August 2, 1918. Because of limited space, the new structural shop at the station was limited to shape and plate shops 100 by 580 feet with a mold loft 120 by 580 feet. The steel storage area was located parallel and adjacent to the building ways. *Courtesy of the U.S. Navy Seabee Museum.*

Coaling plant-weighing house at the U.S. Naval Station Olongapo, Philippine Islands, September 1, 1908. A treaty with Spain gave the U.S. rights to establish naval stations and coaling stations at numerous overseas locations. Established in 1904, the coaling station at Olongapo was one of many fuel depots which fed the Navy's need for high-grade bituminous coal on foreign soil. At that time, the U.S. consumed 350,000 tons of coal annually for its ships. *Courtesy of the U.S. Navy Seabee Museum.*

Photograph of the Marine Guard standing outside the Supply House at Agana, Guam, c. 1924. *Courtesy of the U.S. Navy Seabee Museum.*

Repairs to railroad track on causeway allot, New York Navy Yard, April 3, 1934. *Courtesy of the U.S. Navy Seabee Museum.*

The treaty of 1878 between the United States and Samoa granted to the United States the right to establish a coaling station in Pago Pago Bay for naval and commercial ships. In 1889, the Navy sent a vessel to take possession of the privileges granted by the treaty, to survey the harbor, and determine its fitness for use as a coaling station.

After the Navy, on behalf of the United States, took possession of eastern Samoa, the existing coaling station at Pago Pago Bay was expanded into a full naval station. The island of Tutuila and all other islands of the Samoan group east of longitude 171°W of Greenwich were established into a naval station to be known as the Naval Station Tutuila.

The Tutuila Naval Station served primarily as a supply base until 1940. In 1925, the Navy installed a coal shed with a capacity of 4,500 tons, along with a concrete wharf. A new hydroelectric power plant began operation in 1926 to power the refrigerating and electric lighting machinery. The naval station maintained a complement of 16 officers; 147 enlisted men, including 70 members of the native guard and band; and 6 native seamen for duty in the medical department.

Lt. Commander Paul J. Halloran, who served as the Samoa Public Works Officer, and the American Samoa Construction Committee posing for a photograph after construction of the library was completed in 1938. *Courtesy of the U.S. Navy Seabee Museum.*

Interior and exterior of the American Samoa Library, Pago Pago, Tutuila, Samoa, shortly after construction was completed in 1938. Designed by the Civil Engineer Corps officers in the Public Works Department, the library was made entirely of native materials. *Courtesy of the U.S. Navy Seabee Museum.*

Haitian public works employees working outside the Electric Light Company in Port au-Prince, Republic of Haiti, 1922. In 1915, only three cities—Port au-Prince, Cap-Haitien, and Gonaives—enjoyed the benefit of electric streetlights. Each city received lighting under a concession obtained from the Haitian government prior to the signing of the Treaty. All electric power plants worked by diesel engine, except the hydroelectric plant at Jacmel, and all operated under concession by private owners. *Courtesy of the U.S. Navy Seabee Museum.*

After more than 100 years of instability, coups, and insurrection, numerous British, U.S., and German forces entered Haiti in 1915, ostensibly to protect its citizens from unrest. U.S. Marines and naval personnel stayed until 1934 at the behest of the Republic of Haiti, to support suppression of the reform movement and aid government stability.

The Republic of Haiti, with the assistance of the U.S. Navy and Marine Corps, created a Public Works Administration to further advance its natural resource production, improve sanitation, and develop the public infrastructure. Between 1915 and 1920, the United States and Haiti began negotiations to create a proper public works organization.

Since the Navy's production plan on the island was construction oriented, the Navy directed the Bureau of Yards and Docks to complete the treaty obligations. Navy Civil Engineer Corps officers directed the development of Haitian public works beginning on January 3, 1917. Public works projects included roads, bridges, harbors, public buildings, irrigation, sanitation, and communications. In addition to the eleven members of the Civil Engineer Corps, the staff included an ever-increasing number of Haitian personnel that the officers trained in engineering skills, with the idea being that when the Americans left, the Corps of Haitian Engineers would take over and continue construction work.

Haitian workers excavate the new road system, c. 1922. Prior to 1915, the road system throughout Haiti lacked maintenance and had deteriorated, rendering the roads useless except for animal and foot traffic. By 1923, many improvements to grades, drainages, and surfaces had been finished as part of the U.S. assistance program, which included Navy Civil Engineer Corps officers deploying to Haiti to provide professional assistance. The construction of small bridges and culverts began and workers repaired existing dangerous bridges. *Courtesy of the U.S. Navy Seabee Museum.*

Several bridges in Haiti after local workers completed construction, c. 1922. In 1924, a program of permanent bridge construction was started in Haiti. Standard types of steel truss concrete deck bridges were designed and construction started. The workers repaired 244 bridges and opened 1,725 kilometers of roads to automobile traffic. *Courtesy of the U.S. Navy Seabee Museum.*

View of three 150 horsepower boilers after the base Public Works Department at the Craney Island Fuel Terminal, Virginia, installed them, August 15, 1939. In order to be autonomous, each base had permanent boiler plants installed and placed near the center of the base's industrial section. The boilers contained contemporary modern equipment designed for economical operation. *Courtesy of the U.S. Navy Seabee Museum.*

Fuel oil pump and manifold room at the Craney Island Fuel Terminal, Virginia, August 15, 1939. In addition to fuel storage tanks, Navy Fuel Depots had a system of pumps and piping capable of receiving or dispensing fuel at a rapid rate. *Courtesy of the U.S. Navy Seabee Museum.*

Interior view of the foamite pump house, including bins and hoppers for chemicals, motor driven pump (100 h.p.), and auxiliary driven pump shortly after they were installed at the Craney Island Fuel Terminal, Virginia, August 15, 1939. Foamite was a fire suppressant that formed a bubble blanket of carbon dioxide gas over an oil surface to smother the fire. *Courtesy of the U.S. Navy Seabee Museum.*

Two workers hoist a mounted gun at the Washington Navy Yard, c. 1903. Initially established as a storage and shipbuilding facility, the Washington Navy Yard was re-designated a heavy industrial plant in 1854, primarily concerned with the development, construction, and testing of naval ordnance. *Courtesy of Library of Congress, Frances Benjamin Johnston Collection.*

Photograph of the Washington Navy Yard taken by Brady & Co, June 1866. View looking south towards the north wing of Building 36, which extends from the center to right of the photograph. *Courtesy of the Naval History and Heritage Command.*

Navy recruits outside the barracks at the U.S. Naval Training Station Great Lakes, Michigan, 1913. At the beginning of World War I, the navy immediately needed trained sailors to fill their ranks. In the spring of 1917, only four naval training stations existed in the United States. They had a total capacity of 6,000 men, and the largest in Great Lakes, Illinois, which had accommodations for 3,000 men, opened in 1911. The oldest, in Newport, was commissioned in 1881 and had a capacity for 2,000 men.
Courtesy of the Great Lakes Naval Museum.

In the early days of the Navy, the small administrative department in Washington responsible for managing Navy business was concerned primarily with fleet operations, while the shore establishment, which was of little importance, was neglected. Shore activities eventually took on more added importance once the Navy utilized steam power and replaced sailing ships with the ironclads. As naval materiel took on technical aspects, the Navy needed to expand its shore establishment and the fleet support services available at each base.

In the 1818 Navy Regulations, the Navy first defined the duties of the Commandant of the Navy Yard. The Commandant of the Navy Yard, under the direction of the Secretary of the Navy, employed control over every department in the yard, and was responsible for the maintenance and protection of all buildings, stores, vessels, and for prudent appointment and all labor.

Chapter 5: Base Operations

Photograph of the waterfront area at the U.S. Naval Academy, Annapolis, Maryland, c. 1860-1865. In May 1861, after the Civil War broke out, it became necessary for the Academy to move to Newport, Rhode Island. Ships, including the USS *Constitution*, were employed to transport the officers, families, and any moveable property for the duration of the war. *Courtesy of the National Archives.*

Since the creation of the Navy's shore facilities, it has frequently reviewed and revisited the naval shore establishment administration and industrial system. Three major problems have continually arisen over the years: 1) the retention or selling of particular facilities; 2) internal Navy yard administration; and 3) the liaison between the Navy department and the shore establishment.

On July 1, 1868, Secretary of the Navy Gideon Welles extended the individual Bureau system authority to the navy yards. Under this new system, each Bureau maintained its own private department at each yard and managed its own supplies and materials. This design eliminated the political storekeeper positions, but also led to extreme decentralization. The departments soon developed separate power plants, machine shops, carpenter shops, labor forces, and other industrial shops, which created duplication of expense and effort. It also prevented effective coordinated labor at the yard, as well as a lack of unified central control from either the Commandant or the Navy Department. Each Bureau dealt directly with its own yard departments, and crucial cooperation was often completely lacking. Each Bureau took the best buildings and equipment it could acquire; made its own plans, which may or may not have fit into the plans of its neighbors; and retained independent control of their principal work tools.

Sailors handle electrical cables at the Naval Submarine Base San Pedro battery storage area, 1922. While submerged, contemporary submarines were driven by electric motors on the same shaft as the engines and received their current from storage batteries. Early batteries had open tops which would give off chlorine gas if the acid came in contact with sea water. Later, they were remodeled to close the top and provide for proper ventilation to protect the crew from hydrogen gas. *Courtesy of the National Archives.*

General view of the Philadelphia Naval Asylum, Laning Hall, from the southeast, 1938. The Naval Asylum was a hospital, the Philadelphia Naval School, and a home for retired sailors from 1834 to 1976. The Navy changed the name to the Naval Home in 1889. *Courtesy of Library of Congress, Historic American Buildings Survey Collection.*

Quarters E, F, & G at the New York Navy Yard after workers completed repairs to the cornices, July 10, 1930. Quarters E, F, & G, part of Admiral's Row, is a row of Second Empire style homes formerly used by naval officers at the New York Navy Yard. Some of the homes date back to the Civil War and are located along Flushing Avenue. *Courtesy of the U.S. Navy Seabee Museum.*

First ambulance cart outside the Mare Island Navy Yard stables as its driver harnesses the horses, 1865. The first medical facilities at the Mare Island Navy Yard were located on the sloop-of-war USS *Warren*. The *Warren* arrived in 1854 and remained the main sick bay until 1857, when it was relieved by the USS *Independence*. The *Independence* served as receiving ship and sick bay until 1863, when a temporary hospital was erected in an old granary. *Courtesy of the National Archives.*

For fifteen years no one challenged the Welles decentralization plan. By the early 1880s, with the need to sustain the New Navy, the systemic inefficiency began attracting attention. In an 1883 report, Commodore (later admiral) Stephen Luce recommended a thorough reorganization and centralization for the base mechanical departments. This would place one technical head over all persons engaged in building or repairing ships, over the hull, the machinery, and the equipment. This idea took over thirty-years to complete execution.

The immediate problem regarded civilian labor and the politics surrounding it. The yards, similar to contemporary customhouses and city offices, used the spoils system to hire its civilian labor. Local bosses often dictated the choice of department supervisors, who had charge of hiring workers. Secretary of the Navy William Chandler stated that the Navy could no longer trade the speed of naval engines for political votes. Urgent reform imposed stringent standards for Navy yard labor. The work performed at navy yards required professionals free from the spoils system. In 1891, Secretary of the Navy Benjamin Tracy declared all supervisory positions at the navy yards vacant and set up impartial Efficiency Boards of officers to hire candidates centered on a rigid basis of efficiency. Next, they turned to the workers and rehired every labor position at the yards.

Airship LZ-126 enters the airship hangar at Naval Air Station Lakehurst, New Jersey, for the first time after her flight across the Atlantic from Germany, October 15, 1924. The German government gave the airship to the United States as part of World War I war reparations. The U.S. Navy renamed her USS *Los Angeles* (ZR-3) following delivery. The USS *Los Angeles* (ZR-3) logged a total of 4,398 hours of flight, covered a distance of 172,400 nautical miles (319,300 km), and traveled all over, from the Pacific to the Atlantic. It served as an observatory, an experimental platform, and eventually a training ship for other airships. The USS *Los Angeles* decommissioned in 1932 because of economic measures, but the Navy recommissioned it for a short period after the USS *Akron* crashed in April 1933. The Navy struck it from the active air list in 1939 and dismantled it in its hangar, which ended the longest serving airship's career. *Courtesy of the Naval History and Heritage Command.*

In 1904, the Navy consolidated all facility power units and utility services attached to individual Bureaus under the Bureau of Yards and Docks. This resulted in significant cost savings, which motivated the Navy to consolidate other base activities. In 1908, Naval Constructor Holden A. Evans drew up a comprehensive set of recommendations for coordinating navy yard control and consolidating industrial shops. Knowing the slant towards administrative bottlenecking, Evans sent his report directly to Assistant Secretary Truman Newberry, who later became Secretary of the Navy.

In 1909, Secretary Newberry used many of Evans' recommendations is his General Order No.9. This powerful blow at the yard system stated that all the mechanical departments, yard laborers, building maintenance, and all civil engineering be placed under one division. Under the new plan, the industrial manager was able to reorganize the manufacturing and repair work, as well as reduce the number of shops in order to distribute efficiently the machinery and tools. The commandant remained nominally in control, but with little real supervision over the yard manager. This new system

also mandated the overhauling of the cost accounting system. Budget appropriations still went directly to the Bureaus, but their share of the common facility use had to be pro-rated. This new system failed to take root before Secretary George Meyer replaced Secretary Newberry after President Taft took office.

Later in 1909, after Meyer became Secretary, the Navy hired an outside team of experts to investigate and evaluate all Navy yard activities, specifically the industrial establishment, which included all shops, storehouses, dry docks, wharves, industrial buildings, and all work done in or in connection with the shops. The Navy hired Gantt, Emerson, and Day to investigate the character of work and other services handled at the navy yards; determine which yards properly served the fleet in connection with industrial plants; and assist them in adding scientific management to each of the yards' operations.

Following their advice, the Navy developed a central organization at each yard headed by one officer to develop scientific management and the industrial establishment. The central organization included personnel, Navy yard equipment, public works, administration,

Photograph of the Naval Hospital Reservation Balboa Park, San Diego, shortly after completion, March 8, 1923. The City of San Diego gave the federal government the 17-acre reservation as part of an agreement to bring federal funding and jobs to the San Diego area. The Bureau of Yards and Docks awarded a contract in November 1920 for $718,217.00 to construct six hospital buildings that treated 150 patients. The reservation eventually included 22 buildings that cared for 1,000 patients. *Courtesy of the U.S. Navy Seabee Museum.*

clerical offices, and drafting departments. In 1911, the Navy created the position of "Director of Navy Yards." The office combined the handling of labor, plant improvements, developing new building requirements, and streamlining work methods. The officer in charge answered all questions dealing with shop management, uniformity of methods, comparison of costs and economy, classification of employees, equipment at the yards and shops, and created an analysis of the efficiency of the different navy yards and the actual results obtained. The Navy established the office to improve and unify the management and shop methods at the yards.

The Commandant of the Yard continued to maintain military control of the industrial establishments on the yard and stations. He exercised control of the industrial plant through the mechanical superintendent. All questions arising involving principles of management or of the organization were referred to the Secretary of the Navy. The Commandant of the Yard retained supreme control of every activity at the yard and was the only representative of the Navy department at the yard.

Photograph of Bancroft Hall under construction at the Naval Academy in 1902. Bancroft Hall at the United States Naval Academy in Annapolis, Maryland, is the largest single dormitory in the world. Bancroft Hall, named after former Secretary of the Navy George Bancroft, is home for the entire brigade of 4,000 midshipmen and contains some 1,700 rooms. *Courtesy of U.S. Naval Academy.*

Marine Corps Officers quarters, Building 93 at the New York Navy Yard, December 2, 1925. *Courtesy of the U.S. Navy Seabee Museum.*

View of Quarters "B," looking eastward from Leutze Park prior to World War I at the Washington Navy Yard, District of Columbia, c. 1910. The oldest officer's quarters at the Washington Navy Yard, Quarters B was originally known as the Commander's Quarters, and was the residence of the second officer of the yard. Today it is referred to as Quarters B and has the distinction of being the first permanent building in the Washington Navy Yard. *Courtesy of the Naval History and Heritage Command.*

In 1913, the Navy decided to realign the shore establishment again and issued its new Navy Regulations. The regulations stated that the industrial, public works, inspection, supply, disbursing, accounting, and medical departments remained under the Commandant and Navy yard's purview. The Industrial Department comprised two divisions: the machinery division and the hull division. The commandant remained the general manager of the Industrial department. The shops, manufacturing, and repairing facilities at the Navy yard, excluding those to prepare and manufacture clothing, were assigned to the machinery and hull divisions.

In 1914, the concentrated technical yard control pulled out from under the Director of Navy Yards and returned to the Industrial Manager. Coordination of the shore establishment work during World War I was a minor section under the Assistant for Material in the office of the new Chief of Naval Operations. The Navy yard performance during the war was haphazard at best. There were complaints concerning the slowness of warship repair work and the inefficiency of the Navy yard labor.

Influenza precaution sign mounted on a wood storage crib at the Naval Aircraft Factory, Philadelphia, Pennsylvania, October 19, 1918. Spanish Influenza was extremely active in Philadelphia, with many victims at the Philadelphia Navy Yard and the Naval Aircraft Factory. The sign emphasizes the epidemic's damage to the war effort. *Courtesy of the Naval History and Heritage Command.*

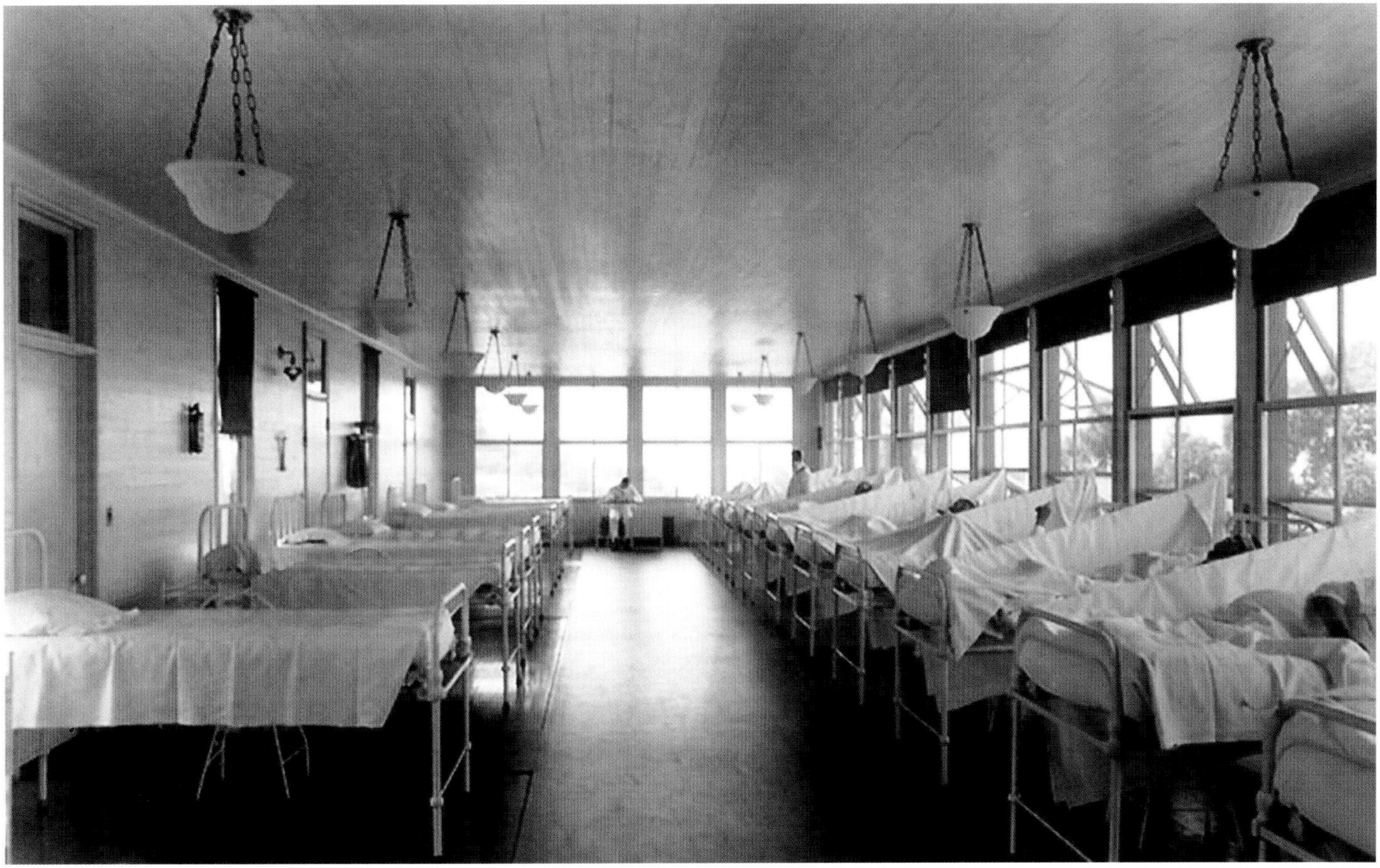

Scene in "D" Ward at the Naval Training Station San Francisco hospital showing sneeze screens erected around beds, c. 1918. Photographed during World War I, probably in the latter part of 1918, when measures were being taken against the spread of influenza. *Courtesy of the Naval History and Heritage Command.*

Sailors of Company D, U.S. Naval Reserve Force, outside the Second Naval District Receiving Barracks at the Newport Receiving Barracks, Rhode Island, 1918. Panoramic photograph was taken by F.H. Farley, Providence, Rhode Island. *Courtesy of the Great Lakes Naval Museum.*

In order to establish a liaison between the department and the shore establishment, the Navy issued General Order No.69 in 1921, to set up the Navy Yard Division under the Assistant Secretary of the Navy. The department head was given the title "Aide for the Navy Yards," later changed to "Director of Navy Yards." Once again, the Navy tried to centralize yard administration, which they believed could be accomplished with minimal additional expense and force. The Bureau of Engineering and the Bureau of Construction and Repair balked. They thought that, since most of the shops at the navy yards were under either one of the two Bureaus, that they should be jointly responsible for the industrial establishment. They alleged that the head of the Navy yard division should report to the Chiefs of the two Bureaus for duty as their assistant; that the division should assume its role as a branch of the Bureaus; and it should not have independent stenographic, clerical, and technical assistants, but rather draw from the Bureaus' forces.

The Director of the Navy Yard position continued to evolve, and the issues continued well into World War II. The Bureaus did not welcome curtailment of their autonomy, and each consolidation or refinement seemed to dwindle, until finally the Navy revised it into a new system. These same issues occurred at the navy yards decade after decade. Numerous proposals and counterproposals were made and many experiments tried. Despite criticisms which advocates of reorganization made, it was an unquestioned fact that during World War II the technical performance of the navy yards, the quantity and quality of work they produced, and their meeting of completion dates was outstanding.

The House Committee on Naval Affairs met in the spring of 1940 and did not report favorably on the alignment and structure of the yards and stations. This resulted in the realignment of the Bureau system, including the merger of the Bureau of Engineering and the Bureau of Construction and Repair into the Bureau of Ships.

New sailors learn their trade in radio class at the U.S. Naval Training Station, Great Lakes, Illinois, c. 1911-1920. These new sailors were some of the first sailors to undergo the new type of navy training system, which included uniformed training and trade schools for the enlisted men showing special aptitude. Prior to this, sailors trained on training ships to learn their trade. *Courtesy of the Great Lakes Naval Museum.*

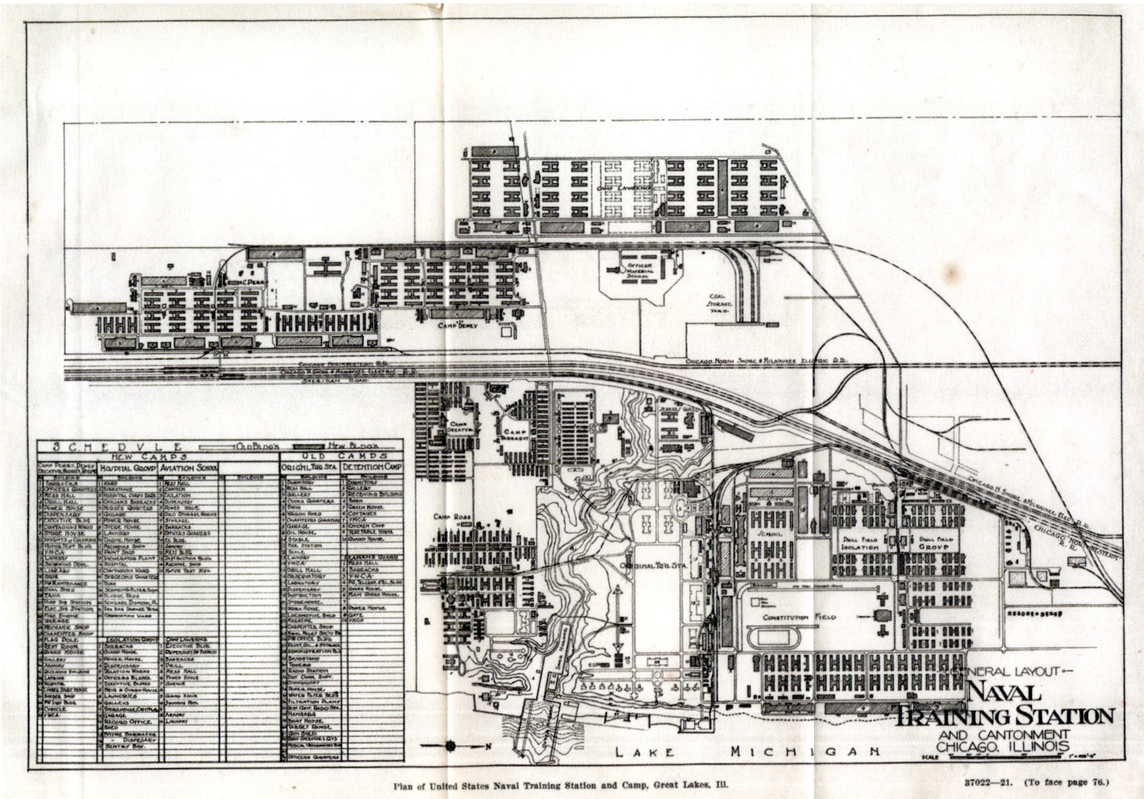

General layout schematic of the Naval Training Station and Cantonment, Great Lakes, Illinois, drawn by the public works officer in 1918. Prior to the war, the Great Lakes Training Station averaged 200 men per month, but reached its zenith in July 1918, when it received 28,000 recruits per month. This rapid increase required massive construction not only at Great Lakes, but also included the creation of 40 additional stations throughout the country to train recruits. *Courtesy of the U.S. Navy Seabee Museum*

View of the Gate House and Marine Barracks at the New York Navy Yard after workers repair the stonework of Gate House and repaint the Marine Barracks, December 3, 1915. *Courtesy of the U.S. Navy Seabee Museum.*

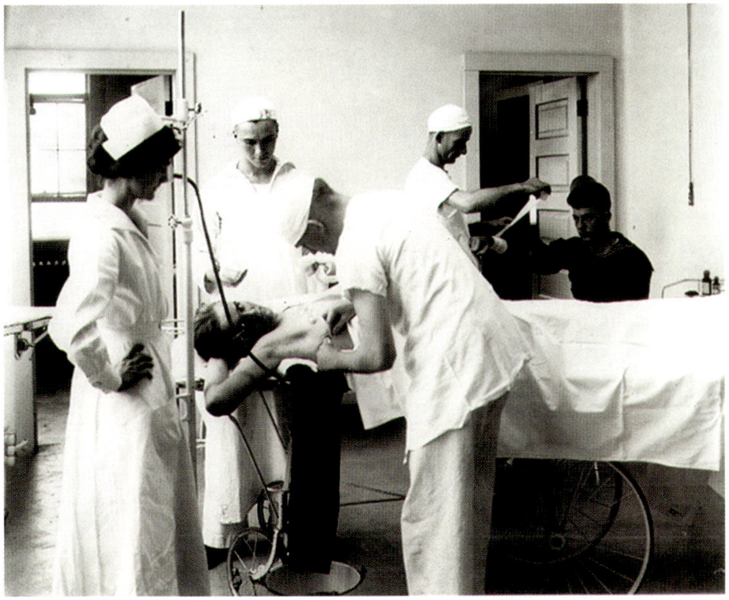

Hospital Corpsman irrigating and dressing wounds under a Nurse's supervision at the U.S. Naval Hospital, New Orleans, Louisiana, c. 1918. The New Orleans Naval Hospital was one of the first emergency hospitals built to care for the wounded and ailing sailors during World War I. The 19 buildings included an administration building, sick officers' quarters, nurses' quarters, operating pavilion, laboratory, laundry, five wards, mess hall, galley, hospital corps barracks, shop building, heating plant, storehouse, and mortuary. *Courtesy of the Naval History and Heritage Command.*

In 1943, the Navy tried again to realign the base facilities and consolidate control. In 1945, the Navy issued General Order No.223 to reorganize once again the shore establishment. The three areas of restructure included centralizing the internal management and technical control of the industrial activities; concentrating authority for the base departmental administration; and integrating the logistical activities under a single command for maximum efficiency. A major change was the discontinuing of the terminology "navy yard" and the creation of a "naval base" in the locality of each navy yard organization, which encompassed the several activities of the navy yards and any additional commands located on the base. The mission of a naval base was to furnish direct services to the operating activities. Each operating activity commanding officer maintained autonomy within their command, but was still under the military command and coordination of the base commandant.

Base operations continue to consist of direct and indirect fleet support, including base administration, public affairs, Marine Corps security, family services, religious services, and public works. Each Navy installation houses separate tenant commands and other Navy support facilities, each having specific and specialized fleet support missions. After more than 200 years of evolution, realignment, and streamlining, the core mission of the shore establishment and base operations remains the same: to support the fleet, the warfighter, and the family.

Photograph of the library and administration building at the Naval Academy, 1873. During 1869, after the Academy returned to Annapolis from Newport, where they were stationed during the Civil War, the Navy converted the first floor of the former Governor's Mansion into the library. *Courtesy of U.S. Naval Academy.*

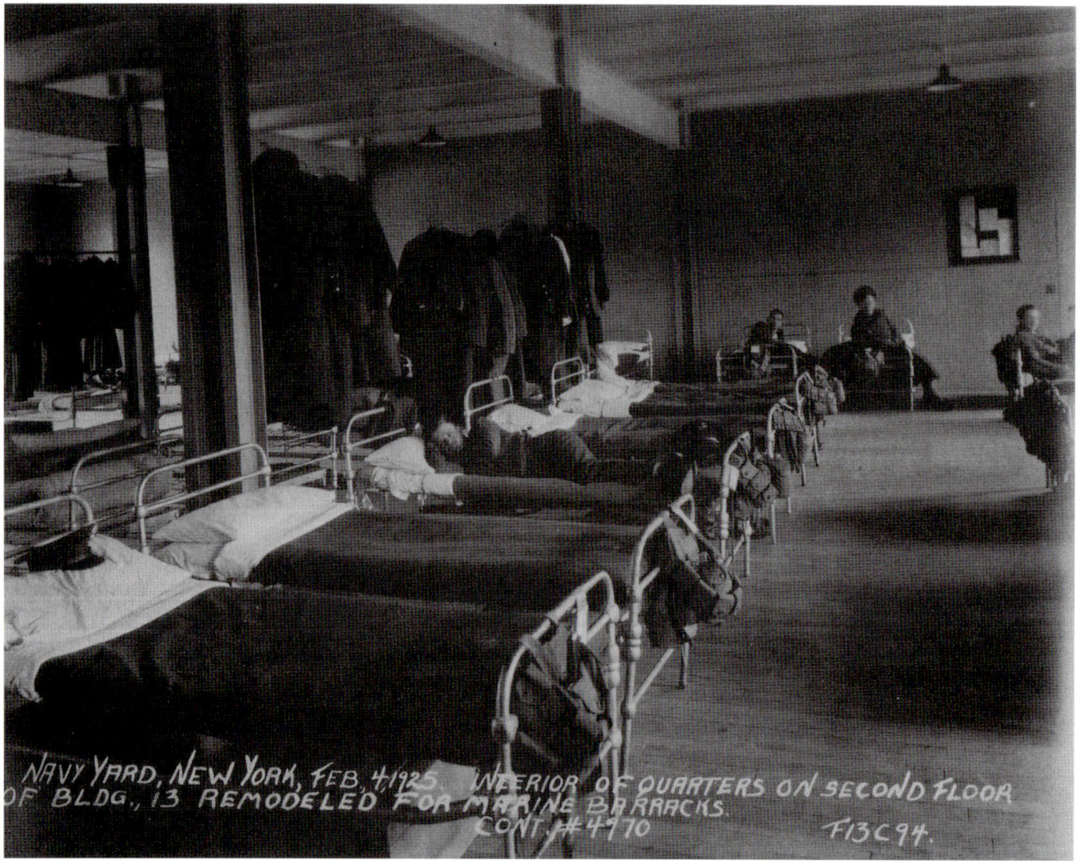

Second floor interior view of Building 13, remodeled for Marine barracks at the New York Navy Yard, February 4, 1925. *Courtesy of the U.S. Navy Seabee Museum.*

Photograph of the Commandant's house at the New York Navy Yard. Quarters A, known as the Commandant's house, was the residence of the commander of the New York Navy Yard. Quarters A is not located on Admiral's Row, but is actually located on Vinegar Hill. It was declared a National Historic Landmark in 1974. *Courtesy of the U.S. Navy Seabee Museum.*

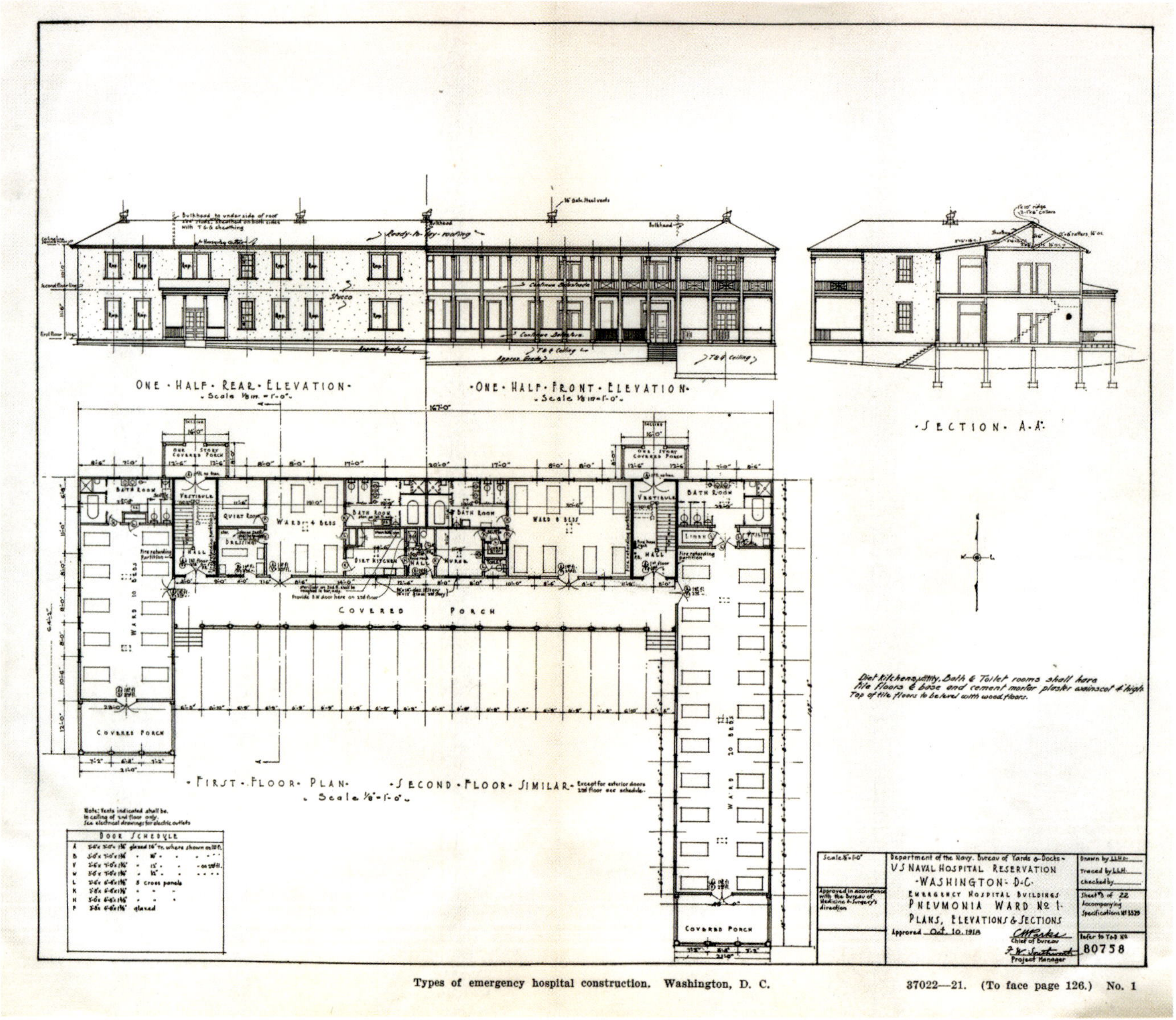

Facilities plan for Pneumonia Ward Number 1 at the U.S. Naval Hospital Reservation, Washington D.C., October 10, 1918. The Observation Ward buildings were designed with deep-screened porches to admit the treatment of pneumonia cases in the outside air. The wards were divided into small wards with easily accessible sterilized rooms, lavatories, and nurses' station. *Courtesy of the U.S. Navy Seabee Museum.*

As the Navy became more a distinct service, it found its hospital system substandard, and the necessity of a separate naval hospital service became evident. In 1798, a law was passed taxing all seamen of the merchant marine 20 cents monthly for the purpose of providing for the care of sick seamen and creating a fund for hospitals. On March 2, 1799, Congress passed an additional act directing the payment of 20 cents monthly from all persons in the naval service for the hospital fund and, in return, they were granted lifetime hospital privileges and care.

During the early 1800s, naval hospital facilities left much to be desired. Only two basic naval hospitals had been built by 1810: one each at Boston and Norfolk. City hospitals attended to infirm sailors at New York, Philadelphia, Savannah, and New Orleans. In other ports private physicians tended to the ailing seamen, and often they were cared for at almshouses, which was charitable housing provided to those in need, including the poor, old, or indigent. In February 1811, Congress passed legislation authorizing the establishment of Navy hospitals. Navy personnel funded the hospitals through a standard pay deduction. By the late 1820s, sites had been purchased for permanent naval hospitals at Boston, New York, Philadelphia, and Norfolk. The Naval Asylum – later called the Naval Home – in Philadelphia was completed in 1834, and was the first home and hospital constructed for indigent and elderly naval personnel.

Wherever there is a naval station of any importance, the Navy builds a dispensary or hospital to care for the health of all naval personnel and their families. Starting in 1842, the Bureau of Yards and Docks designed all the necessary buildings for the hospitals. The building's structural requirements included appropriate materials and construction in accordance with the local climate conditions. This demanded preliminary investigations, surveys, and a set of standard plans.

Navy hospital facilities, especially Veterans' accommodations, increased after World War I. The returning wounded and disabled service members overburdened existing facilities. In 1922, as part of the second Langley Bill, the federal government appropriated $17 million towards the construction of hospitals for World War veterans. The Bureau of Yards and Docks prepared drawings and specifications for a series of new hospitals to service the men. The Bureau constructed these facilities at Tupper Lake, New York; Gulfport, Mississippi; Excelsior Springs, Missouri; Augusta, Georgia; and St. Cloud, Minnesota. In November 1920, construction began on six hospital buildings on the Naval Hospital Reservation, Balboa Park, California. The six original buildings were designed to care for 150 patients. Another major development in the evolution of naval hospitals occurred in the 1930s, which included a new hospital in Philadelphia to replace two aging naval facilities, and a new medical center was built at Bethesda, Maryland.

U.S. Naval Ambulance Ship *Solace* berthed at the Mare Island Navy Yard, California, 1901. The USS *Solace* was the first Navy ship to fly the Geneva Red Cross flag. *Solace* was commissioned April 14, 1898. Able to accommodate 200 wounded sailors, she was protected by the articles of the Geneva Convention while flying the Red Cross flag. *Courtesy of the National Archives.*

View of the Naval Training Camp at Mare Island Navy Yard, California, with ships laid up in reserve along the waterfront in the middle distance, c. 1920-21. Early in April 1917, Mare Island only had a capacity for 600 recruits that were housed in the seamen's barracks and receiving ship moored at the yard. At the beginning of World War I, the Bureau of Navigation requested that temporary barracks be erected to house 5,000 men at the newly designated training camp. *Courtesy of the Naval History and Heritage Command Donation of Rear Admiral Ammen Farenholt, USN.*

Marine Barracks at the Pensacola Navy Yard, August 15, 1888 (l to r): view of the commander's office, kitchen, mess room, and tailor and barber shop; and paint shop, carpenter's cool house, library, wash house, bathroom, and officers' water closet at the Pensacola Navy Yard. *Courtesy of the Naval History and Heritage Command.*

Officers pose for a photograph outside the Flying School Office at the Naval Aeronautic Station, Pensacola, Florida, c. 1915. In January 1914, the Navy facility at Pensacola, all but abandoned after a major hurricane in 1906 and a yellow fever epidemic in 1908, was re-designated a Naval Aeronautic Station. The first naval aviation unit assigned to Pensacola consisted of nine officers, less than two dozen enlisted men, and eleven diverse airplanes. *Courtesy of the Naval History and Heritage Command and Lieutenant Rodman Dekay, Jr., USNR.*

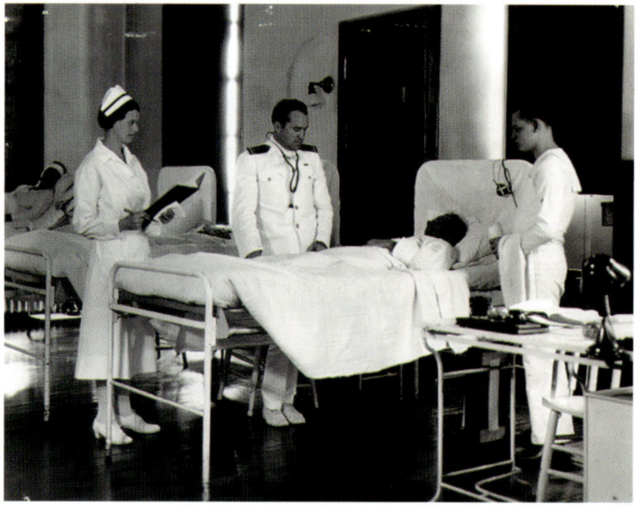

Ward scene during the 1930s, with a Navy doctor, nurse, and corpsman attending to a patient at the U.S. Naval Hospital, Washington, D.C. *Courtesy of the Naval History and Heritage Command, Nursing Division, Bureau of Medicine and Surgery.*

New Marine draftees arriving for instruction at the Marine Corps Recruit Depot, Parris Island, South Carolina, 1919. A set of Marine barracks are in the background. *Courtesy of the U.S. Navy Seabee Museum.*

African-American barracks, latrine, and mess hall at the Charleston Navy Yard, South Carolina, June 2, 1919. Mobilization of reserves and volunteers at the navy yard overcrowded the receiving ship and other accommodations, which required the construction of a small tent city in early 1917 to house all the incoming personnel. The temporary barracks for 1,000 men began construction on April 30th and finished on June 3, 1917. *Courtesy of the U.S. Navy Seabee Museum.*

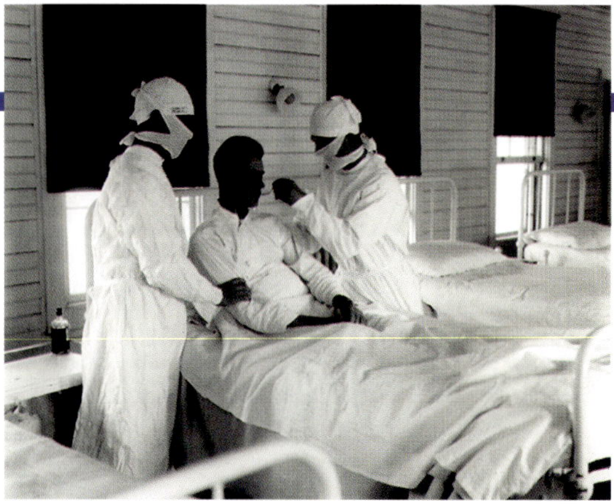

Masked medical personnel treat to an influenza patient at the U.S. Naval Hospital, New Orleans, Louisiana, c. Autumn 1918. *Courtesy of the Naval History and Heritage Command.*

This 1933 aerial photograph shows the Naval Hospital Balboa in San Diego, California, after several additional buildings were constructed. Originally created as a tent dispensary in 1917, the hospital was later enlarged to a major complex in 1922 to care for the Pacific Fleet. *Courtesy of the U.S. Navy Seabee Museum.*

Officer's quarters at the Boston Navy Yard, Massachusetts, 1874. *Courtesy of the U.S. Navy Seabee Museum.*

Officers from the seaplane NC-1 photographed on May 3, 1919, prior to their trans-Atlantic flight attempt (l to r): LCDR Patrick N.L. Bellinger; LCDR Marc A. Mitscher; and Lt. Louis T. Bairn. Bellinger commanded the squadron of seaplanes making the first trans-Atlantic flight. On May 8, 1919, NC-1, NC-3, and NC-4 took off from Naval Air Station Rockaway, Long Island, New York. Bellinger's plane (NC-1) sank shortly after takeoff. For his leadership of the flight he was awarded the Navy Cross. *Courtesy of the Naval History and Heritage Command.*

Permanent bases for naval aviation in the United States began in Pensacola, Florida, in 1914. The Bureau of Yards and Docks designed and constructed all shore facilities for naval aviation, both heavier-than-air and lighter-than-air, including facilities for the Naval Reserve. The Bureau of Yards and Docks, in conjunction with the Bureau of Aeronautics, helped create a program for air base development.

In 1913, aviation pioneer Captain Washington Irving Chambers established the first mobile naval aviation camp. The mobile naval aviation group trained at the newly constructed airfield at Greenbury Point, which was just outside the Naval Academy in Annapolis. It became immediately apparent that the cleared space was too small for land planes, the site was too close to the Naval Academy's rifle range, and the water was too shallow for hydroplanes. As a result, the mobile naval aviation group inaugurated a second camp at Guantanamo Bay, Cuba, during the winter of 1913. At that time, the aviation camps consisted of a few portable tents, a beach, and a sheltered body of water. Usually it worked in cooperation with a naval vessel specialty detail, which maintained the camp's equipment.

A Navy board investigated the primitive air program in 1913 and recommended a formal air department be established to train pilots, acquire planes, and establish a new aeronautical station. In January 1914, the Navy facility at Pensacola, all but abandoned after a major hurricane in 1906 and a yellow fever epidemic in 1908, was re-designated a Naval Aeronautic Station. The first naval aviation unit assigned to Pensacola consisted of nine officers, less than two dozen enlisted men, and eleven airplanes.

Naval air bases require large and unique structures, including hangars, shops, and storehouses, as well as ramps and runways for seaplanes and amphibious vessels. The Bureau of Yards and Docks and the Bureau of Aeronautics conducted a significant portion of this early innovative work without precedence or guidelines. These early advancements often supplied valuable information to municipalities and local industries towards the growth of private aeronautics industries.

When the United States joined World War I on April 6, 1917, the Navy had 38 pilots, 163 aviation assistants, and 54 airplanes, though none was capable of or equipped for war service. Pensacola remained the only naval air station in the country, although its facilities were limited, consisting of only three steel seaplane hangars, a brick structure used as a hangar, an airship shed mounted on a barge, and a few service buildings.

Photograph of the USS *Macon* (ZRS-5) under construction in the Goodyear-Zeppelin Corporation hangar at Akron, Ohio, c. early 1933. The sister ship of the USS *Akron* (ZRS-4), she first flew in April 1933, a few weeks after the *Akron* was lost at sea in a tragic storm. *Courtesy of the Naval History and Heritage Command.*

Station carpenters at the Naval Training Station, Newport, Rhode Island, during World War I.
Courtesy of the U.S. Navy Seabee Museum.

During the war, the Bureau of Yards and Docks constructed thirteen naval air facilities from Nova Scotia to Panama to guard the coast against German submarines. By the end of World War I, the Navy had built forty-four naval air installations in Europe. The Navy also developed an air station in San Diego to cover all aspects of naval training and operations. Located at North Island within the bay, its permanent facilities were largely developed postwar, though plans were prepared and the first large contract was let several months before the armistice. Early accommodations provided for 1,000 student aviators and 50 officers, with hangar and shop facilities for 20 or more seaplanes, one airship, and two kite balloons.

Prior to the war, a program to construct lighter-than-air craft had been undertaken and a contract to fabricate eight airship steel hangars was authorized. The use of the dirigible as an offensive weapon during the war resulted in the construction of the Navy's first lighter-than-air station at Lakehurst, New Jersey, in 1921. During the war, an Army-Navy Airship Board convened to study the potential use for lighter-than-air craft. The Board gave jurisdiction over the development of rigid dirigibles to the Navy, and the Army transferred Camp Kendrick at Lakehurst, New Jersey, to the Navy for testing, training, and berthing of the dirigibles.

Marine Barracks near the Washington Navy Yard, District of Columbia, 1936. Marine Barracks, Washington, D.C., is located at 8th and I Streets, Southeast, in Washington, D.C. Established in 1801, it is a National Historic Landmark, the oldest post in the United States Marine Corps, the official residence of the Commandant of the Marine Corps since 1806, and the main ceremonial grounds for the Marine Corps. *Courtesy of the U.S. Navy Seabee Museum.*

USS *Akron* (ZRS-4) moored near the airship hangar at Naval Air Station Lakehurst, c. 1933. The USS *Akron* (ZRS-4) was lost in a weather-related accident off the New Jersey coast early on April 4, 1933, killing 73 of the 76 crew and passengers. *Courtesy of the Naval History and Heritage Command.*

Naval Air Station Lakehurst underwent a massive construction program in the early 1920s that included the building of several hangars, a powerhouse, permanent quarters, a gas cell shop, storage buildings, and an experimental mobile telescopic dirigible mooring mast. Hangar 1 at NAS Lakehurst was an unprecedented structure at 258 feet wide and 800 feet long, with a maximum clear height of 172 feet. The hangar was sufficient to house the dirigibles *Los Angeles* and *Akron*, as well as several smaller airships simultaneously. Never before had so large an enclosure been constructed without intermediate supports, and the pioneer work of the Bureau of Yards and Docks helped in the development of designs for other large dirigible hangars for the Navy and other commercial interests.

Together the Bureau of Yards and Docks and the Bureau of Aeronautics developed mooring masts and mechanical handling devices for docking and un-docking dirigibles. Masts were either fixed or mobile. Fixed masts were constructed of structural steel or were guyed, deriving its name from using guy wires. Mobile masts operated over the ground on crawler treads or on railroad tracks.

Officers and enlisted men from the Public Works Department at Naval Training Station, Coasters Harbor Island, Newport, Rhode Island, September 1921. During World War I, the public works department was increased to boost production and provide additional facilities for the handling and storage of spare parts and reserve supplies. *Courtesy of the U.S. Navy Seabee Museum.*

In the years between the world wars aviation facilities steadily expanded. Two developments somewhat strengthened naval aviation growth during the 1930s. Eight naval reserve air bases were set up at several points throughout the United States, and three air stations were constructed on the West Coast to accommodate the transfer of the Fleet's main strength to the Pacific. The three West Coast stations included Seattle, WA; Alameda, CA; and San Pedro, CA.

Although air stations had many missions to perform, and many facilities, such as hangars, seaplane ramps, and barracks, to aid in the performance of their mission, they had one basic mission – to keep the aircraft flying. All maintenance, from minor corrections for wear and tear to major overhaul, needed to be performed on the ground by mechanical personnel. Ground crews needed housing and aircraft needed maintenance on the ground.

Bird's eye view shows the barracks and men exercising on the grinder at the New York Navy Yard with the harbor and Williamsburg Bridge in the background, 1909. *Courtesy of the Library of Congress.*

Photograph of the wood working shop at the Naval Submarine Base, Los Angeles, 1922. *Courtesy of the National Archives.*

Sailors work on torpedoes at the torpedo storage building at the Naval Submarine Base, Los Angeles, 1922. The Bureau of Yards and Docks, in consultation with the Bureau of Ordnance, designed standard torpedo storehouses, with or without overhaul space, and standard warhead storehouses. Standard racks were designed during World War I to increase the capacity of the storehouse and permit the handling of any one torpedo without moving the others. *Courtesy of the National Archives.*

Interior photograph of the Naval Submarine Base Los Angeles electrical room after workers installed the new system in 1922. The dampness which is constantly present at a Navy base had a deteriorating effect upon any insulating materials. The seawater and electrolytic conductor was particularly damaging to electrical wiring and equipment at naval facilities. The severity of it led the Bureau of Engineering to be particularly rigid and exacting in the matter of specifications for the manufacture, testing, and installation of naval electrical equipment. This created a very high grade and efficient machinery and appliances. *Courtesy of the National Archives.*

Marine guard stands outside the Wapping Street entrance at the Boston Navy Yard. In 1800, the Charlestown Navy Yard in Massachusetts was established, and the first detachment of Marines arrived from other duties in the Boston area. They took up guard details and established one of the oldest Marine Barracks in the United States. The Marine presence continued at the navy yard until 1973, when the yard was officially closed as a military installation. *Courtesy of the Naval History and Heritage Command.*

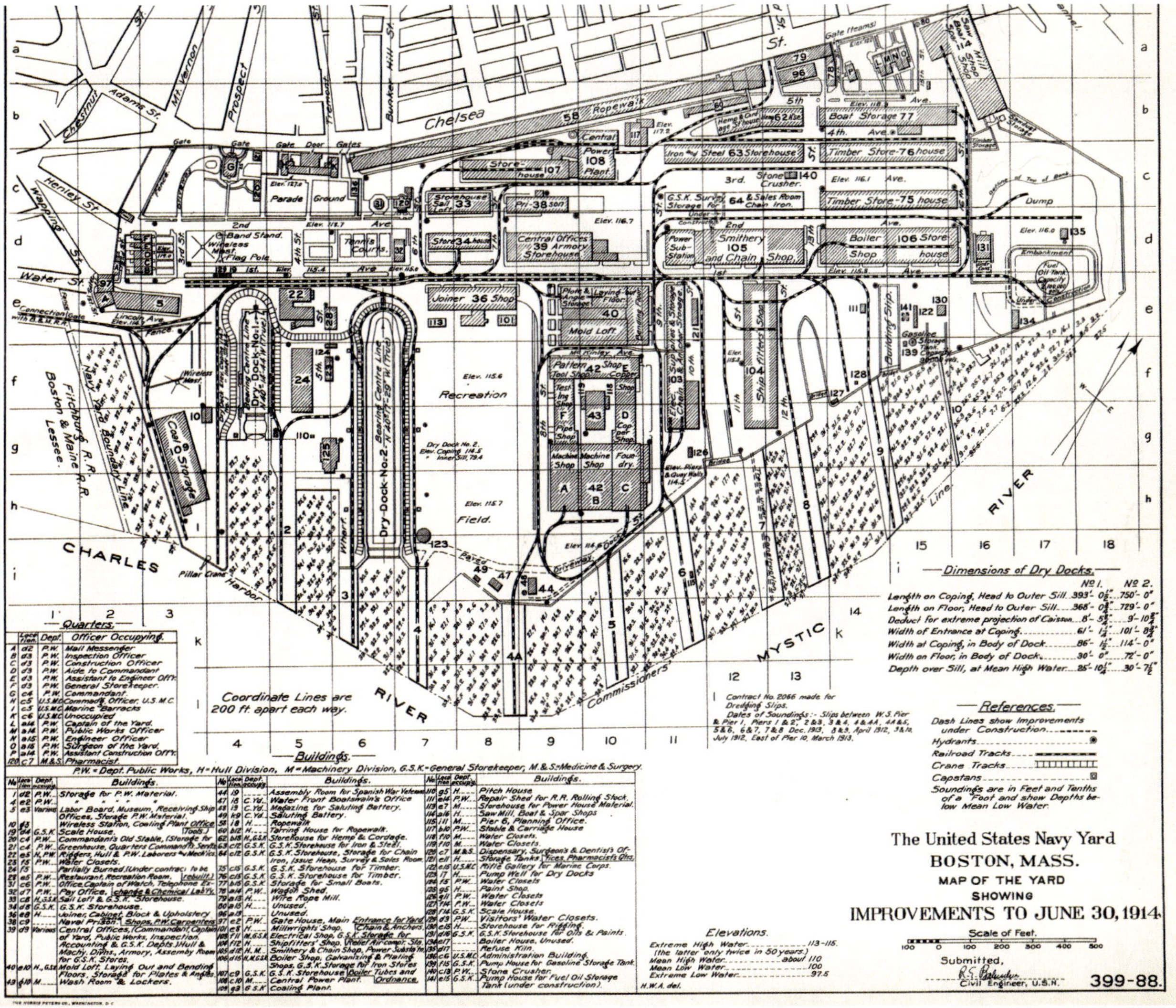

Facilities plan of the Boston Navy Yard created by the Public Works officer LCDR Reuben Bakenhus, CEC, USN, and approved by the Bureau of Yards and Docks, June 30, 1914. *Courtesy of the U.S. Navy Seabee Museum.*

In 1938, the Navy had only 1,000 planes. With the passage of the Vinson Act and the Two-Ocean Navy Bill, the number grew to its final prewar figure of 27,500. However, these aircraft lacked enough facilities to care properly for them. The Hepburn Board, created to survey the shore establishment and its prewar status, stated that the need for additional shore facilities for aircraft far exceeded that for other craft. The shore establishment failed to keep pace with earlier authorizations for materiel, aircraft, and vessels, and was woefully ill prepared for the global war ahead.

Photograph of the Naval Hospital at Portsmouth Navy Yard from across the river. The first naval hospital at Portsmouth was established in 1834 in an old building built in 1802, which had been occupied by the Lieutenant of the Yard. The Navy remodeled the building at a small expense as a temporary hospital for the station that could accommodate 10 patients. The hospital cared for the sick and wounded of the Navy in all wars of the United States since its establishment. *Courtesy of the U.S. Navy Seabee Museum.*

Waterfront industrial area at the Puget Sound Naval Shipyard with the battleships USS *Idaho*, USS *New Mexico*, USS *Oklahoma*, and USS *Arizona* docked at the piers, and with the USS *Saratoga* in dry dock, December 18, 1936. Prior to World War II, Puget Sound was the only battleship repair yard on the Pacific coast. Its facilities included three dry docks and four piers, one of which mounted a 250-ton hammerhead crane. *Courtesy of the U.S. Navy Seabee Museum.*

Photograph of the Commandant's residence at the Mare Island Navy Yard, California, c. 1901. *Courtesy of the U.S. Navy Seabee Museum.*

Photograph of the Naval Hospital on Guam taken by the public works officer during his deployment to the island, c. 1920. In August 1910, the Schroeder Hospital and the land around it was ceded to the U. S. Government and a new building for the Susana Hospital Women's and Children's ward was completed. Together with the Schroeder Hospital, the two merged to become the Naval Hospital, Guam, and were unique, in that it was the only U. S. Naval Hospital in existence with a women's and children's ward. *Courtesy of the U.S. Navy Seabee Museum.*

The Commodore's house at the Memphis Navy Yard, Tennessee, c. 1850.
Courtesy of the Naval History and Heritage Command.

View of the east end of the Charleston Navy Yard, June 2, 1919. At the outbreak of World War I, mobilization of naval personnel overcrowded the receiving ship, requiring new housing for the incoming men. The city of Charleston tendered the free use of land just outside the navy yard to extend the new 1,000-man camp to accommodate 5,000 men. The increase in yard activities associated with World War I necessitated considerable new construction, including draining the marshland, building barracks, industrial shops, and administration buildings. *Courtesy of the U.S. Navy Seabee Museum.*

U.S. Veterans Hospital in St. Cloud, Minnesota, schematic that was designed by the Bureau of Yards and Docks, c. 1918. Navy hospital facilities, especially Veteran's accommodations, increased after World War I. The returning wounded and disabled servicemen overburdened existing facilities, and the Veteran's Bureau requested that the Bureau of Yards and Docks plan and build a series of new hospitals to service the men. *Courtesy of the U.S. Navy Seabee Museum.*

Construction workers erecting emergency hospital, Building "E," at the U.S. Naval Hospital, New York Navy Yard, March 24, 1919. The hospital buildings at the New York Navy Yard were two and three stories in height, with reinforced concrete frame, floors, and roofs with stuccoed *terra cotta* walls. The emergency hospitals had large wards designed to care for 40 patients in order to handle the large patient load for war service. *Courtesy of the U.S. Navy Seabee Museum.*

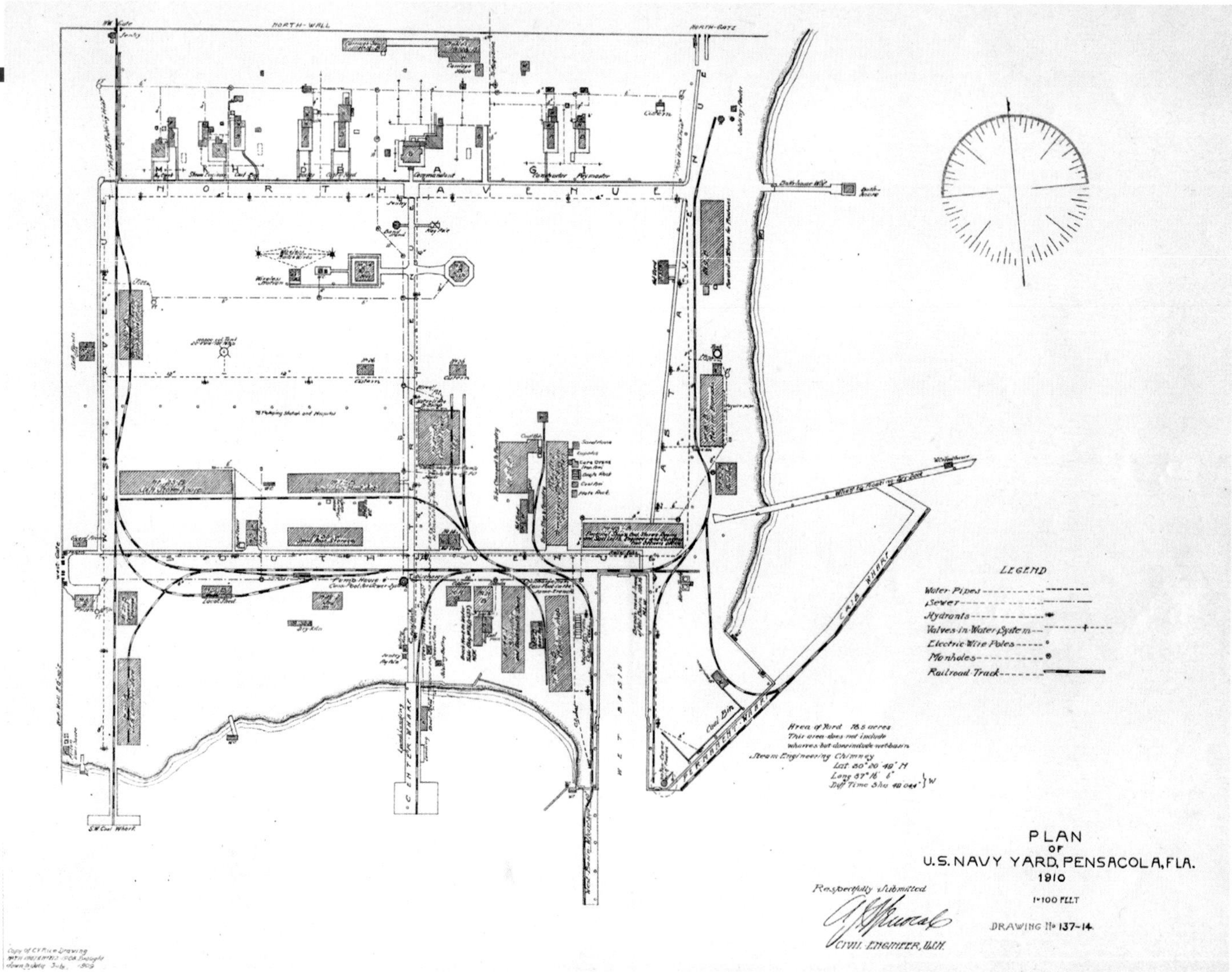

Facilities plan of the U.S. Navy Yard, Pensacola, Florida, designed in 1910. The Pensacola Navy Yard was established in 1826 and remained an important naval base on the Gulf Coast throughout the early Mexican-American, Civil, and the Spanish-American Wars. However, the yard closed in 1911 after the 1906 hurricane and tidal wave destroyed many of the base structures and the 1908 yellow fever epidemic raged through the area. After remaining in caretaker status for more than two years, the Navy chose the base as the Navy's first flying school and aviation facility in 1914. Early in 1913, the navy established the first mobile naval aviation camp just outside Annapolis, and later that year moved it to Guantanamo Bay, Cuba. At that time aviation camps were little more than a few portable tents, a beach, and a protected body of water. The camps consisted of two or three planes with a makeshift machine shop to create custom materiel. Personnel included an instructor, a student or two, and a couple of mechanics. The aviation camps also worked in cooperation with a naval vessel specially detailed to provide support facilities. In April 1917, Pensacola was the only naval air station in the country. Its facilities, though capable, consisted only of three steel seaplane hangars, a brick structure used as a hangar, an airship shed mounted on a barge, and a few service buildings. *Courtesy of the U.S. Navy Seabee Museum.*

View of the truck owned by the U.S. Naval Medical Supply Depot, Brooklyn, New York, c. 1935. In 1850, the United States Navy established the Naval Medical Supply Depot in Brooklyn with Medical Department Officers serving as Medical Materiel Managers. On May 26, 1905, a new depot was established on the grounds of the Naval Hospital in Brooklyn. Between 1905 and 1941, naval expansion and the preparation for war required the construction of several other buildings for the depot. *Courtesy of the U.S. Navy Seabee Museum.*

Photograph of Danny and his carabao, a species of domesticated water buffalo, at the Naval Station Cavite, c. 1902-1910. Starting in 1902, Danny and his carabao began working at Naval Station Cavite hauling heavy debris and material around the base. Danny was the first worker at the base designated under the schedule of wages with the rating "Laborer with Carabao." The carabao died in 1910 and was buried deep in the yard parade ground. *Courtesy of the U.S. Navy Seabee Museum.*

Group photograph of the first twenty Navy nurses, known as the "Sacred Twenty," at the Naval Hospital, Washington, D.C., October 1908. In May 1908, at the behest of the Chief of the Bureau of Medicine and Surgery, Congress authorized the establishment of a female Nurse Corps within the United States Navy. By October, these first twenty women had been appointed to the Corps and were preparing for their initial assignments at several naval hospitals. *Courtesy of the Naval History and Heritage Command.*

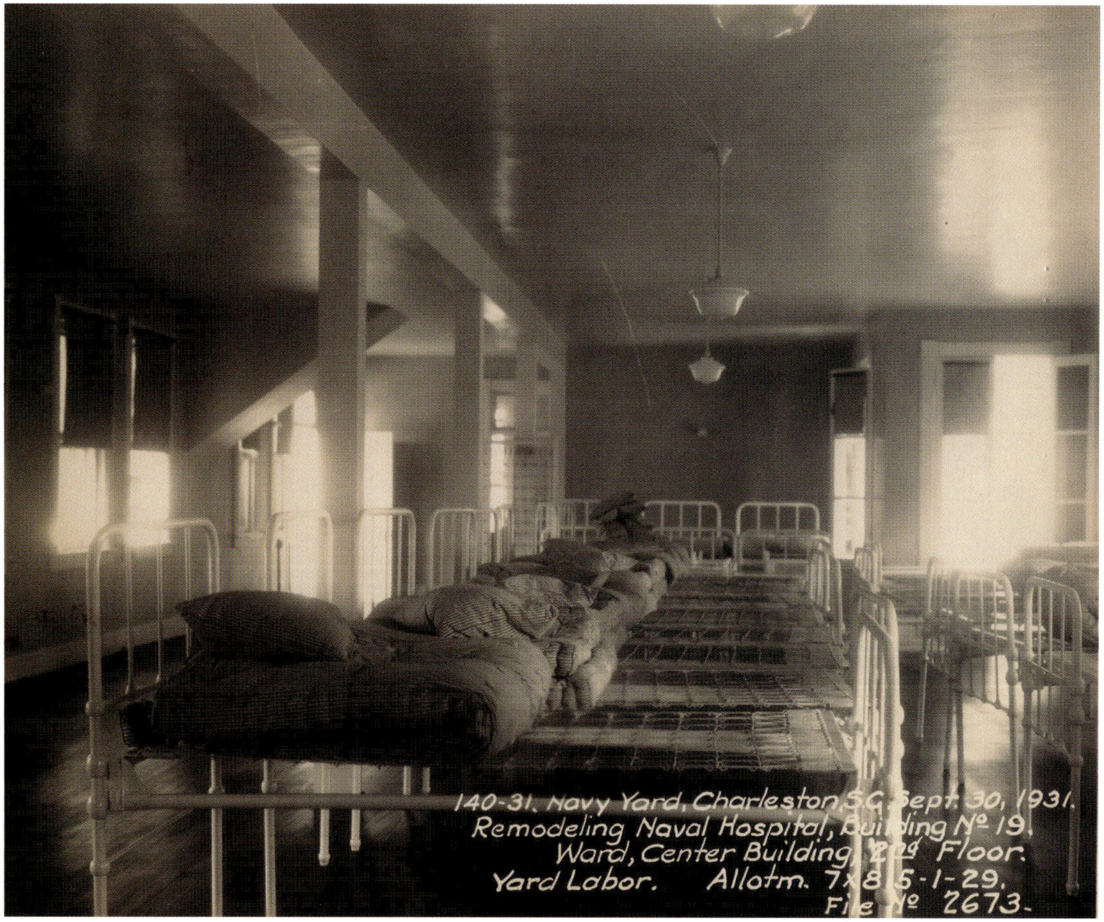

Photograph of the newly remodeled Ward Building 19, 2nd Floor, U.S. Naval Hospital, Charleston, South Carolina, September 30, 1931. *Courtesy of the U.S. Navy Seabee Museum.*

Photograph of the Physics Laboratory at the U.S. Naval Academy, Annapolis, Maryland, 1889. *Courtesy of the U.S. Navy Seabee Museum.*

"Oklahoma" Officers quarters at the U.S. Naval Academy, Annapolis, Maryland, 1893. *Courtesy of the U.S. Navy Seabee Museum.*

Sailors attend class at the Naval Training Station Great Lakes, Illinois, c. 1915. Great Lakes Training Station opened in 1911 with accommodation for 3,000 men and an initial capacity of 1,500 recruits. The training station was established as the result of a demand for a more scientific recruit training compared to the old training produced on ships. *Courtesy of the Great Lakes Naval Museum.*

View of the armory at the U.S. Naval Academy, Annapolis, 1889. *Courtesy of the U.S. Navy Seabee Museum.*

Midshipmen and families attend graduation in Dahlgren Hall, U.S. Naval Academy, Annapolis, Maryland, 1922. Construction began on Dahlgren Hall in 1899, and was designed by New York master architect Ernest Flagg, who was educated at the Ecole Des Beaux Arts in Paris, France. *Courtesy of U.S. Naval Academy.*

Midshipmen eating in the Naval Academy mess in 1889. The midshipmen were divided into mess crews, with each commanded by a first and second captain. Each crew had a specific table, and each midshipman had a particular seat, with the captains at the head and foot of the table. *Courtesy of U.S. Naval Academy.*

Yeomen (F) at the U.S. Naval Hospital, Mare Island Navy Yard, California, January 1918. Yeoman (F) was a rank in the U.S. Naval Reserve in World War I for female sailors. Typically, female Yeoman reservists performed clerical duties, such as typing, telephone operation, bookkeeping, stenography, inventory control, and accounting. *Courtesy of the Naval History and Heritage Command, Rear Admiral Ammen C. Farrenholt, USN (MC) Collection.*

Photograph of Hangar One at the Naval Air Station Lakehurst, New Jersey, built by the Bureau of Yards and Docks. Hangar One, at one time or another, served as home for every airship in the Navy, as well as the *Graf Zepplin* and *Hindenberg*. In 1921, the Navy established the Lakehurst Naval Air Station to serve as its headquarters for lighter-than-air flight. The new base became the center for experimentation and development of rigid airships for strategic and commercial purposes, as well as the control station for all naval lighter-than-air flights. The first major facility at Lakehurst was Hangar Number 1, a gigantic structure built in 1921 to house the huge helium-filled dirigibles. Hangar Number 1 measures 961 feet long, 350 feet wide, and 200 feet high. At each end are two pairs of massive steel doors, mounted on railroad tracks. These double doors are structurally separate from the hangar itself. Each door weighs 1,350 tons and is powered by two 20 horsepower motors, although provisions were made to open the doors manually, which required nine men to accomplish. *Courtesy of the U.S. Navy Seabee Museum.*

Remodeling Building 19 for a lavatory at the U.S. Naval Hospital, Charleston, South Carolina, August 31, 1931. *Courtesy of the U.S. Navy Seabee Museum.*

Workers install hangar doors for a straight-truss type Seaplane Hangar at the Coastal Air Station, Cape May, New Jersey, December 3, 1917. Upon declaration of war, the possibility of submarine depredations and the effectiveness of air patrols as a protective measure led to the immediate establishment of air patrol stations at strategic points on the Atlantic coast. *Courtesy of the U.S. Navy Seabee Museum.*

Officers, nurses, and enlisted men on the hospital staff, U.S. Naval Hospital, Great Lakes, Illinois, c. 1924-1927. Captain Ammen C. Farenholt, USN(MC), Hospital Commanding Officer, is seated in the front row, center. *Courtesy of the Naval History and Heritage Command, Rear Admiral Ammen C. Farenholt collection*

View of the main portion of the New London Submarine Base from south of Quarters "D" looking southwest, July 2, 1928. Early in 1916, the Navy decided to transform the Naval Coaling Station New London into the first continental base chosen to be a submarine base. The extensive improvements included construction of a wharf paralleling the shoreline, barracks, water tanks, coal shed, storehouses, and a powerhouse. *Courtesy of the U.S. Navy Seabee Museum.*

The submarine has a long history in the United States, beginning with the *Alligator* – although never commissioned – which the Union towed to South Carolina for use in the capture of Charleston. The *Alligator* was lost due to bad weather April 2, 1863, off Cape Hatteras, North Carolina. Meanwhile, the Confederates shipped the CSS *Hunley*, a Confederate States of America submarine, by rail to South Carolina on August 12, 1863, to defend Charleston. On February 17, 1864, the *Hunley* attacked and sank the USS *Housatonic* in Charleston harbor, becoming the first submarine to sink an enemy ship, but sank soon after, drowning all eight crew members.

The first major progress in submarines began in the late nineteenth century with the building of the USS *Holland* (SS-1). The *Holland*, named after John Philip Holland, was a pioneer craft in service for 10 years, and conducted developmental and trial vessel service for many systems on other early submarines. The submarine really came of age in World War I.

Prior to the outbreak of World War I, the Navy devoted very little thought to the care and upkeep of submarines, except at the primary yards and stations. The submarine crews lived in mother ships that provided sleeping accommodations and, to some extent, machine-shop

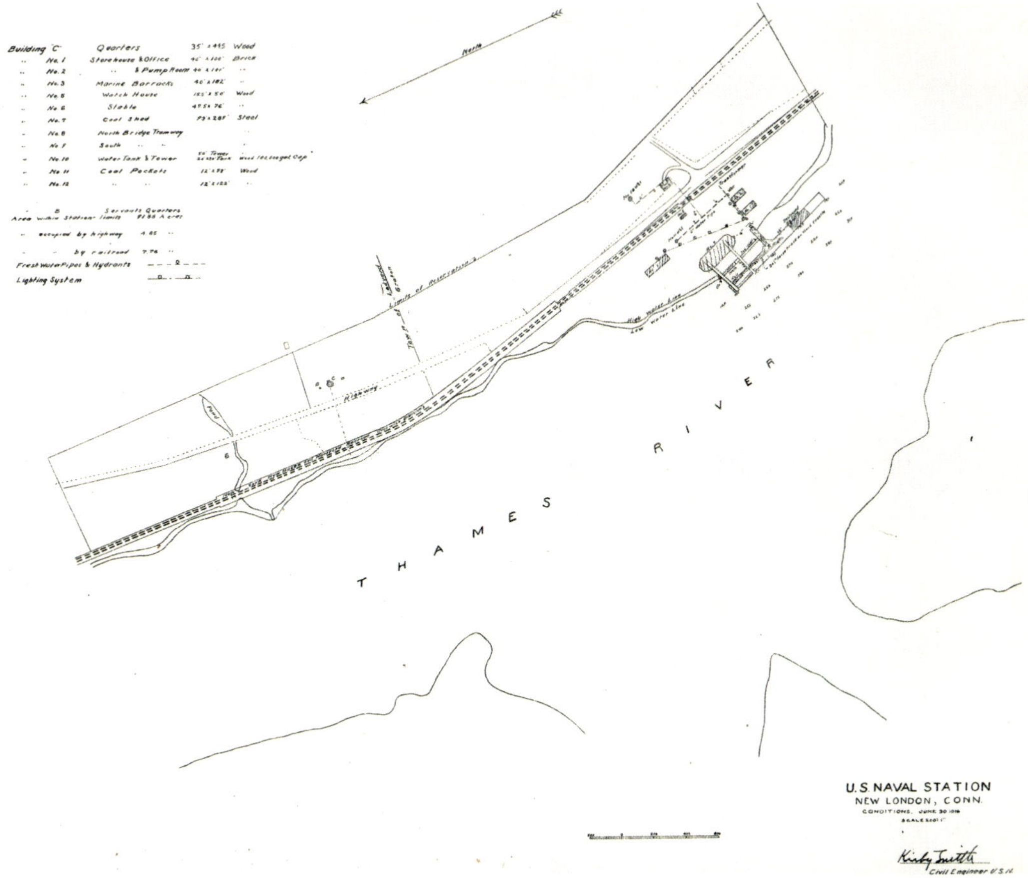

Facilities plan of New London Submarine Base drawn by Lieutenant Kirby Smith, CEC, USN, June 30, 1916. Beginning in 1915, the Bureau of Yards and Docks conducted studies on developing a submarine base. The base needed to be self-sustaining, with shop facilities, storage facilities, berthing for submarines, and barracks for crews and officers. The base also required radio communication towers, fresh water, fuel supplies, a small magazine for ordnance, and industrial shops. *Courtesy of the U.S. Navy Seabee Museum.*

equipment. Most of the submarine repair jobs done at the navy yards were conducted in shops provided for general purposes, and the actual work was completed by a member of the crew and yard machinists. Naval leadership did not consider establishing bases dedicated to the maintenance of submarine detachments outside of the established navy yards, and no comprehensive plan had been worked out for the accommodations of submarine units.

In June 1915, the Bureau of Yards and Docks commenced studies with a view towards developing the first submarine base that would have machine shops, storage facilities, berthing spaces, and barracks for crews and officers dedicated entirely towards the submarine detachments. The new base plan included two piers to be constructed approximately 250 feet apart to berth a unit of ten submarines. It had the ability to berth two submarines on each side of both piers, leaving space for a tender and sufficient space for future increases in the number of submarines home ported at the base by triple banking.

The Gas Works at the U.S. Naval Academy, c. 1860. The need for housing was so great at the academy during the Civil War that the blacksmith shop was converted into quarters for eight students. This rustic cantonment was nicknamed the "Gas House" in honor of its occupants, who were reputed to be Annapolis' most avid conversationalists. *Courtesy of U.S. Naval Academy.*

Group photograph shows instructors from the Diving School, Class of June 1917, at the Naval Torpedo Station, Newport, Rhode Island. The Navy's Diving School was established in Newport in approximately 1916-1917, but was later disestablished in the early 1920s due to cutbacks. The Navy School of Diving and Salvage was reestablished at the Washington Navy Yard in 1927 when it was realized that only 20 Navy divers were trained to dive more than 90 feet. *Courtesy of the Naval History and Heritage Command and Mrs. J.V. Tibbals.*

The *Hindenburg* alongside ZMC-2, a Navy dirigible, in Hangar One at the Naval Air Station, Lakehurst, New Jersey, c. 1936. The Deutsche Zeppelin-Reedere Company completed construction of the *Hindenburg* in early 1936 and placed her in operation to transport passengers across the Pacific. The *Hindenburg* completed 17 round trips across the Atlantic Ocean in 1936, its only full year of service, with 10 trips to the U.S. and seven to Brazil. After making its first South American flight of the 1937 season in late March, the *Hindenburg* left Frankfurt for Lakehurst, New Jersey, on the evening of May 3rd on its first scheduled round trip between Europe and the United States that year. Although strong headwinds slowed the crossing, the flight had otherwise proceeded routinely as it approached for a landing three days later. Around 7:00 p.m. local time on May 6th, at an altitude of 650 feet (200 m), the *Hindenburg* approached Naval Air Station Lakehurst and prepared to land. At 7:25, the airship caught fire and engulfed in flames in only 37 seconds. The location of the initial fire, the source of ignition, and the initial source of fuel remain subjects of debate. Of the 36 passengers and 61 crew members on board, 13 passengers and 22 crew members died, as well as one member of the ground crew. *Courtesy of the U.S. Navy Seabee Museum.*

View of several buildings and a pier along the waterfront area at the U.S. Naval Academy, Annapolis, Maryland, c. 1869, looking northeast from the tower of "New Quarters." The twin turret monitor moored in the Severn River, at left, is the USS *Tonawanda* (renamed *Amphitrite* in 1869). The ships at the pier in the right center are the USS *Dale* and USS *Santee*. *Courtesy of the Naval History and Heritage Command.*

The Navy commissioned New London, Connecticut, as the first continental submarine base in December 1915. During the construction program of World War I, the Bureau of Yards and Docks built eight finger piers in New London, together with storehouses, shops, and barracks, raising the number of buildings to forty-three. Other submarine stations were soon established at Pearl Harbor, Hawaii; Coco Solo, Panama; and Hampton Roads, Virginia.

The conversion to submarine bases came just in time. Soon America was caught up in World War I, and the submarine bases rapidly expanded to keep up with wartime demands for submarines and crews. During World War I, submarines were outfitted, serviced, and home ported at New London, and more than 10,000 officers and men were trained there for the new "Silent Service." Naval Submarine Base New London remained the Navy's only station specially equipped for the training of submarine personnel until Congress approved the Hepburn Report recommendations in 1939.

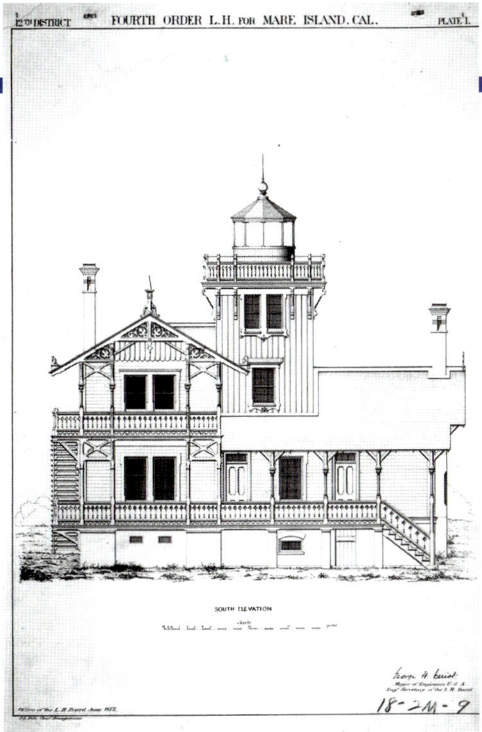

Sketch of the Mare Island Lighthouse from the south, drawn in June 1872 by George Elliot, Major of Engineers, Engineering Secretary of the I.H. Board. Built in 1873, the Mare Island Lighthouse was perched high on a hill with a supply pier below. The site was abandoned in 1917 and was razed in the 1930s. *Courtesy of the National Archives.*

Sketch of the U.S. Naval Academy in Annapolis, Maryland, drawn c. 1853. This wood engraving is of a drawing by W. R. Miller, published in March 1853 in *Illustrated News*, New York, New York. *Courtesy of U.S. Naval Academy.*

The Hepburn Report included the construction of additional submarine bases at Wake Island, Midway Island, and Guam; Kodiak and Sitka, Alaska; and San Juan, Puerto Rico. The Bureau of Yards and Docks designed, built, and maintained all these structures for the Bureau of Ships. The Bureau also built over 200 additional training facilities at the Submarine Base New London to train the elite submarine force. Submarine Base New London trained thousands of submariners to serve in both the Atlantic and Pacific Theaters. One out of every five U.S. Navy submarines paid the ultimate sacrifice during World War II.

Building 142, a lighter-than-air dirigible hangar constructed at the Naval Air Station Pensacola, Florida, August 25, 1939. Prior to the outbreak of war, eight dirigible hangars were contracted to be erected at designated locations along the U.S. coastline, including one at Pensacola. These steel airship hangars were approximately 250 feet long and 133 feet wide, and had a clearance of 66 feet. *Courtesy of the U.S. Navy Seabee Museum.*

Union Officers at the Commandant of the Yard's quarters, Quarters B, at the Washington Navy Yard, District of Columbia, c. 1862-1864. When officers of the 71st New York Regiment required lodging in the capital, which was already crowded with military, Lieutenant John Adolphus Dahlgren (later Rear Admiral) gave them his accommodations in the Commandant's House. He moved to Building 1 for the remainder of the war, where he slept and dined in the room opposite his office. *Courtesy of the Naval History and Heritage Command.*

Concept design for the Naval Medical Center, Bethesda, Maryland, that was drawn by the Bureau of Yards and Docks in 1938. The original Naval Medical Center at Bethesda consisted of the Naval Hospital, designed to hold 1,200 beds; the Naval Medical School; the Naval Dental School (now the National Naval Dental Center); and the Naval Medical Research Institute. *Courtesy of the U.S. Navy Seabee Museum.*

Quarters for the Civil Engineer Corps officers located at Agana, Guam, c. 1924. The bachelor officer's quarters were located on the second floor of this structure and offered only basic accommodations. *Courtesy of the U.S. Navy Seabee Museum.*

Interior view of the Naval Air Station Lakehurst airship hangar, c. 1931. The Navy awarded the construction contract for the hangar to the Lord Construction Company on September 8, 1919. Hangar One consists of three pinned, arched steel trusses supported on steel towers. The outer columns and chords support the sidewall framing and siding. Shops, offices, and service areas were built on each side along the entire length of the hangar on the mezzanine level. *Courtesy of the U.S. Navy Seabee Museum.*

USS *Shenandoah* (ZR-1) undergoing repairs inside the airship hangar at Naval Air Station Lakehurst, New Jersey, 1924. This photograph, taken by Clements, shows her forward framework and arrangement of gas cells and fuel tanks in her lower hull. *Courtesy of the Naval History and Heritage Command, Collection of Admiral Thomas C. Kinkaid, USN.*

Naval Fuel Depot located at the South Boston pier, February 5, 1919. The gradual reduction in petroleum supplies just prior to World War I compelled the Navy to build large fuel storage facilities at various key points along the coasts to hold in reserve adequate supplies secured from Mexican oil fields. *Courtesy of the U.S. Navy Seabee Museum.*

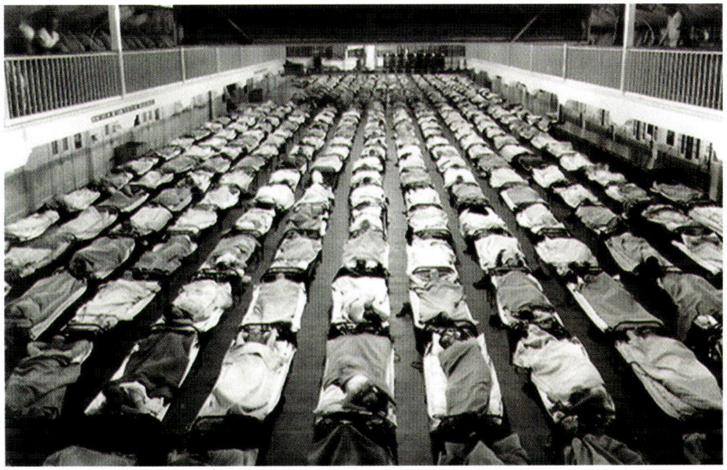

View of a crowded sleeping area on the drill hall floor of the main barracks at Naval Training Station San Francisco, California, c. World War I. The camp at San Francisco was established to temporarily relieve overcrowding at other stations. After some minor repairs and equipage, a variety of buildings were used to house incoming trainees. Eventually the Navy erected a tent camp to house the overflow of enlisted personnel. *Courtesy of the Naval History and Heritage Command.*

View of Moffett Field's "Hangar One" built during the Depression era for the USS *Macon*. Constructed on a network of steel girders sheathed with galvanized steel, the airship hangar rested firmly upon reinforced pads anchored to concrete pilings. The hangar's clamshell doors were designed to reduce turbulence when the Macon moved in and out on windy days. The doors weigh 200 tons each and operate on their own 150 horsepower motors via an electrical control panel. *Courtesy of the U.S. Navy Seabee Museum.*

View of the office, barracks, latrine, and mess hall at the Charleston Naval Fuel Depot, January 2, 1919. *Courtesy of the U.S. Navy Seabee Museum.*

Marine guards stand in formation outside the Marine barracks at the U.S. Naval Academy, Annapolis, Maryland, c. late 1890s. In 1870, the Marine Station at the Naval Academy was made a permanent post. Every morning at 9 a.m. there was a dress parade and guard mounting by the Marines. There was also a daily drill in the forenoon on weekdays. *Courtesy of the U.S. Navy Seabee Museum.*

One of the first battalions at the Marine Corps Officers School, Port Royal Naval Station, South Carolina, 1909. In 1883 the Navy, seeking a location for a new base to control the "gray market" on the Southern East Coast, purchased land on Parris Island to build a new naval station. The base opened in 1889, and was used intermittently by the Navy until just before the Spanish-American War. On March 3, 1901, the naval station at Port Royal was placed in caretaker status and construction began in Charleston, South Carolina, to build a new modern station. The base remained in caretaker status until 1909, when the Marine Corps established an Officers' School of Application at the old naval station. The Navy turned the facility over to the Marine Corps later that year, and on November 1, 1915, it was renamed Marine Corps Recruit Depot Parris Island. *Courtesy of the U.S. Navy Seabee Museum.*

Photograph of one of the naval hospital wards in Washington, D.C., built under emergency status to provide facilities for about 300 patients, 1918. The Washington Naval Hospital was constructed, furnished, and equipped in 60 calendar days in order to accommodate the thousands of wounded and infirm returning from Europe. The structures comprised two observation wards, two general wards, a subsistence building, and a powerhouse. *Courtesy of the U.S. Navy Seabee Museum.*

View of the Naval Air Training Station San Diego from the south, June 20, 1923. The Naval Air Training Station, San Diego, provided housing for 1,000 student aviators and 50 officers, with hangar and shop facilities for 20 or more seaplanes, 1 airship, and 2 kite balloons. *Courtesy of the U.S. Navy Seabee Museum.*

View of early construction at the Naval Air Station San Diego, June 26, 1923. The first Naval Air Station San Diego master plan included developing the city into the largest naval center on the West coast that could provide for every phase of naval training and operations. The permanent facilities represented largely post-World War I development, though plans were prepared and the first large contract was awarded several months before the armistice. *Courtesy of the U.S. Navy Seabee Museum.*

U.S.

The USS *Akron* (ZRS-4) moored at Naval Airbase Sunnyvale, California (later renamed Moffett Field), c. May 1932. The Bureau of Yards and Docks and the Bureau of Aeronautics jointly developed mooring masts and mechanical handling devices for docking and undocking dirigibles. Masts were either fixed or mobile. The fixed masts were constructed of structural steel or were guyed, deriving its name from using guy wires. Mobile masts operated over the ground on crawler treads or on railroad tracks. *Courtesy of the Naval History and Heritage Command.*

View of several navy airships at Naval Air Station Lakehurst, New Jersey, c. 1930s. The use of the dirigible as an offensive weapon during World War I resulted in the construction of the Navy's first lighter-than-air station at Lakehurst, New Jersey, in 1921. During the war, an Army-Navy Airship Board convened to study the potential use for lighter-than-air craft. The Navy was given jurisdiction over the development of rigid dirigibles, and the Army transferred Camp Kendrick at Lakehurst, New Jersey, to the Navy for testing, training, and berthing of dirigibles. *Courtesy of the U.S. Navy Seabee Museum.*

Northwest bay structural shop at the Norfolk Navy Yard from the southwest, February 11, 1918. At 300 feet wide and 700 feet long, the design divided the shop into three longitudinal aisles 100 feet wide, each serving as smithery and boiler shop, shape shop, and plate shop to increase efficiency. *Courtesy of the U.S. Navy Seabee Museum.*

Pay car trailer at the New York Navy Yard, September 29, 1921. Each yard and base distributed pay to the civilian and military personnel in cash twice a month. This pay trailer moved around the base to pre-set locations with armed Marine escorts. *Courtesy of the U.S. Navy Seabee Museum.*

Shipbuilding Ways at the Boston Navy Yard built in 1934 as part of the National Industrial Recovery Act (NIRA). Due to administrative action restricting expenditures from naval appropriations, public works construction almost stopped completely during the early Depression years. However, funds were allocated to the Navy under the NIRA for public works construction projects around the country. These funds were used by the Navy to hire American workers, get them back to work, and help stabilize the economy. *Courtesy of the U.S. Navy Seabee Museum.*

General interior view of the foundry shop looking northwest at the Philadelphia Navy Yard, June 2, 1919. The building construction included inclined sidewalls of steel sash and glass for the main bay, and continuous top-hung ventilation sash for the upper portion in lieu of the usual enclosed design. *Courtesy of the U.S. Navy Seabee Museum.*

Ship's boilers for the USS *Craven* under construction in the Erecting Shop at the Norfolk Navy Yard, Virginia, May 15, 1917. *Courtesy of the Naval History and Heritage Command.*

Foundry department employees pour molten metal into molds at the Mare Island Navy Yard, September 1937. The typical foundry building comprised a high center aisle 80 feet wide with two lower side aisles, one 55 feet wide with a mezzanine floor, and one 45 feet wide, as well as a 100 foot material and flask yard adjacent to the latter. The civilian personnel molded, poured, and handled the castings in the center aisle. *Courtesy of the National Archives.*

Foundry Department members sit for a photograph at the Mare Island Navy Yard, California, 1901. In 1891, Secretary Benjamin Tracy eliminated the spoils system and rehired all civilian personnel based on a rigid efficiency rating scale. *Courtesy of the National Archives.*

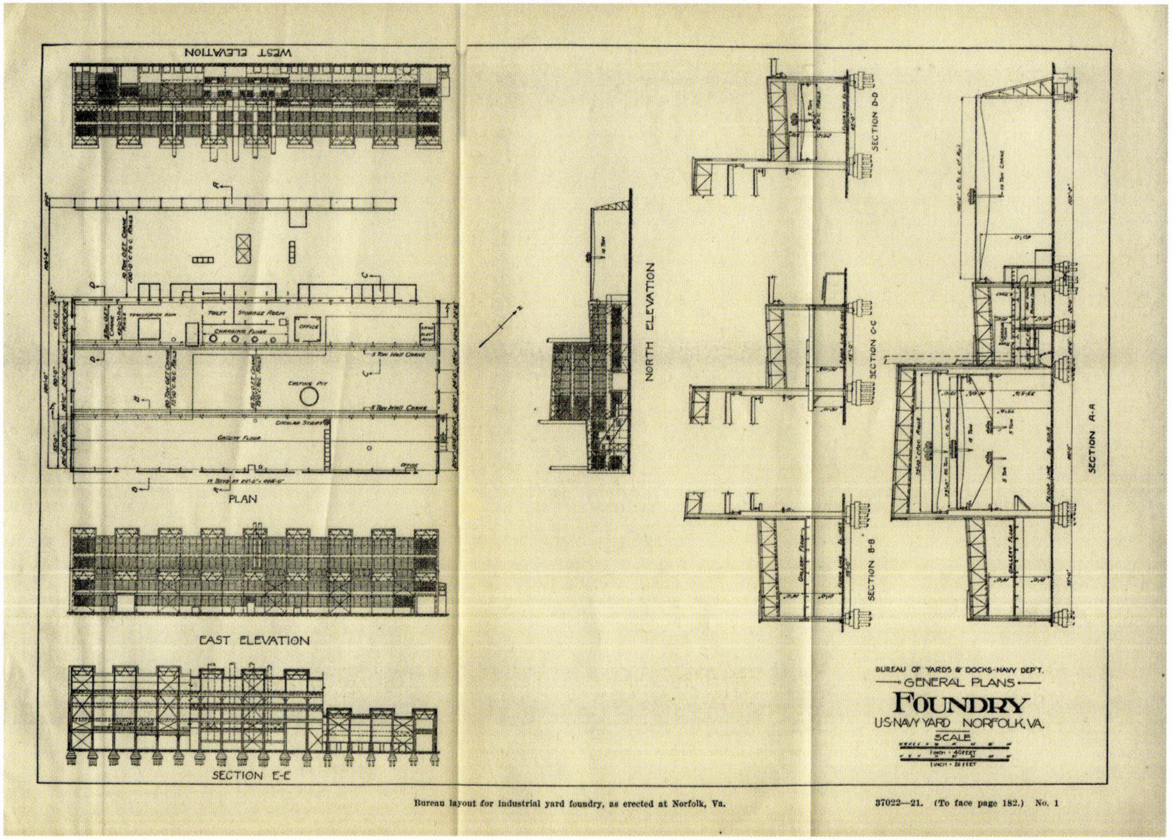

General plans for the industrial yard foundry at the Norfolk Navy Yard, Virginia, 1917. In the 1820s, the growing use of steam power in navy yards allowed them to purchase machinery to work with metals. The brass and bronze foundries, the molding lofts, and their accompanying machine shops were equipped with mechanical lathes, boring machines, drills, presses, shapers, bending machines, cutting machines, and buffers. *Courtesy of the U.S. Navy Seabee Museum.*

View of the west bay of the Norfolk Navy Yard foundry, February 6, 1919. The iron foundry at the Norfolk Navy Yard was capable of casting engine blocks, boring and finishing them, manufacturing pistons of close tolerances, and fabricating entire iron hulls, complete engines, and auxiliary machinery. *Courtesy of the U.S. Navy Seabee Museum.*

The submarine USS *G-2* berthed at a finger pier, probably at the New York Navy Yard just prior to World War I. The Navy placed the *G-2* in full commission at the New York Navy Yard on February 6, 1915. *Courtesy of the Naval History and Heritage Command.*

Workers planking lifeboats in the small boat shop at the Philadelphia Navy Yard, Pennsylvania, October 28, 1918. World War I accelerated Philadelphia's conversion into a modern ship construction and repair yard. In 1918, the boat shop received an 80- by 400-feet by 46-foot high addition to its structure. The shop also had two 15-ton traveling bridge cranes installed to reposition the boats mechanically. *Courtesy of the National Archives.*

USS *Thrasher* (SS-26), later renamed *G-4*, while docked in Philadelphia, October 2, 1912. The *G-4* was fitted out at the William Cramp & Sons shipyard, Philadelphia, Pennsylvania, on October 2, 1912. *Courtesy of the National Archives.*

View of the pump house at the Naval Submarine Base, Coco Solo, Canal Zone, August 23, 1939. The War Department designated Coco Solo Point as a new site for a submarine base on May 25, 1917. The Bureau of Yards and Docks constructed the base for the maintenance and upkeep of 20 submarines. *Courtesy of the U.S. Navy Seabee Museum.*

View of the marine railway machine foundation under construction at the Charleston Navy Yard, South Carolina, January 13, 1919. Two new building ways and a marine railway were completed in June 1919, advancing Charleston's future as a first-class navy yard. *Courtesy of the U.S. Navy Seabee Museum.*

Receiving ship at the Puget Sound Naval Shipyard pier, March, 16, 1923. Shortly after Congress declared war, the Navy brought the USS *Philadelphia* to the Puget Sound Naval Shipyard and used her as a receiving ship to quarter up to 1,600 recruits. Additionally, the base erected a tent camp to house 5,000 men until personnel completed the barracks. *Courtesy of the National Archives.*

View of the Smithery in Building 11 at the New York Navy Yard while undergoing repairs to bottom exterior walls, August 31, 1915. The Smithery, or Blacksmith's shop, created objects from iron or steel by forging the metal. Blacksmiths produced wrought iron gates, grills, railings, light fixtures, furniture, sculpture, tools, agricultural implements, cooking utensils, horseshoes, and weapons for the navy yards. One of the most import tasks for a navy yard was to remain independent and maintain the ability to create most tools and materiel required by the fleet and yard. *Courtesy of the U.S. Navy Seabee Museum.*

Staff of the Pattern and Joiner shops, c. 1905, at the Naval Gun Factory, Washington Navy Yard. The pattern shop building was four stories high,with the lower three made of reinforced concrete flat-slab construction used for the storage of patterns. The upper story was of steel framework with adequate daylight, ventilation, and heating, and a light crane for shop purposes. *Courtesy of the Naval History and Heritage Command, Mrs. Janet T. Ryon, and Lawrence Gichner Collections.*

Photograph of the metal shop at the Naval Submarine Base, San Pedro, California, in 1922. From 1919 to 1922, a submarine base was located on Pier 1, Outer Harbor, Long Beach, California, and was an outgrowth of a Reserve Force Naval Training Station established in 1917. Rear Admiral Arthur J. Helms recommended San Pedro as one of three sites for a submarine base on the West Coast. In 1920 and 1921, approximately 1,340 men overhauled H and I type submarines at San Pedro, but by 1929 the base began specializing in servicing auxiliary ships and the submarine duties were transferred. *Courtesy of the National Archives.*

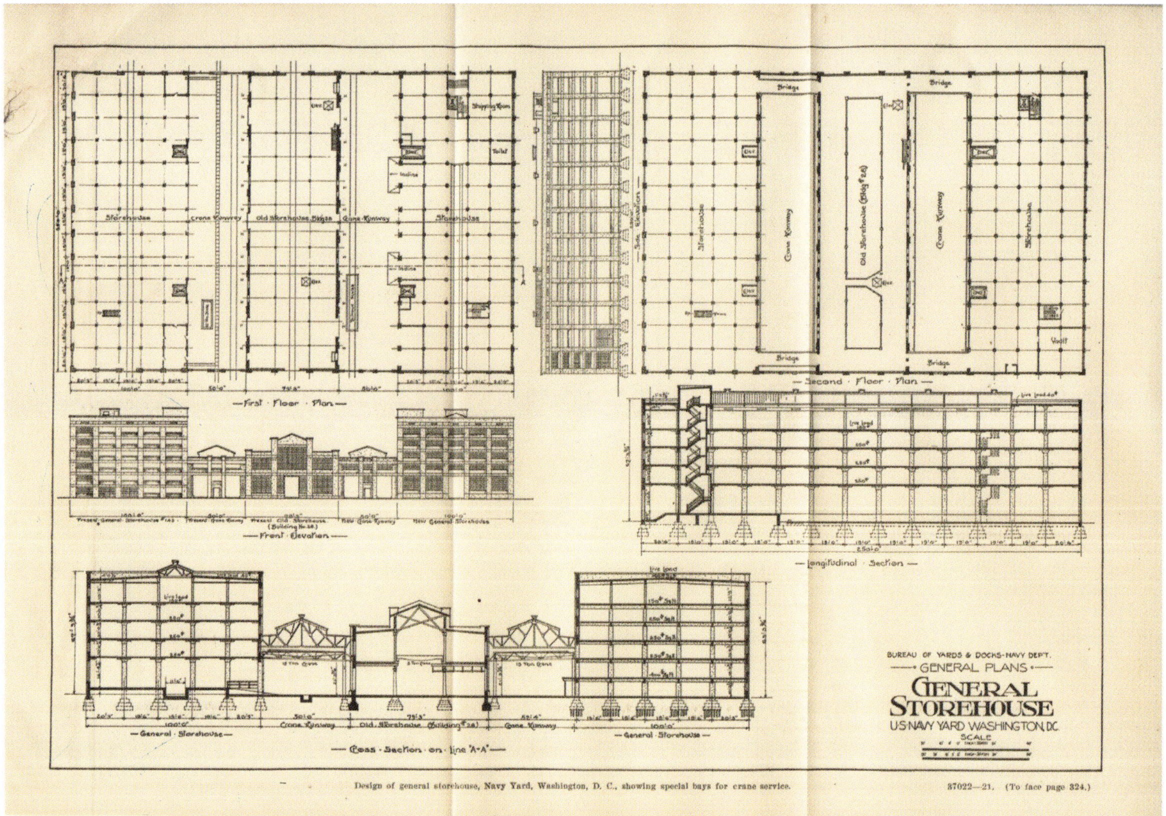

General plans for a General Storehouse at the Washington Navy Yard, designed by the Bureau of Yards and Docks in 1917. At the outbreak of World War I, the Navy required an extensive number of large reinforced concrete storehouses for the industrial yards and main stations. Many of the bases required millions of square feet of additional space to store supplies for the fleet. Additional construction included large cold storage and ice manufacturing plants to store perishable materials for the expanding military personnel. *Courtesy of the U.S. Navy Seabee Museum.*

Storage bins and paint and oil storehouse at the Naval Submarine Base, Coco Solo, Canal Zone, August 8, 1939. The Coco Solo Naval Submarine Base was established in 1917 on a 130-acre peninsula between Margarita Bay and Manzanillo Bay in the Canal Zone. The base underwent a modernization update starting in 1940 as a result of the Hepburn Board decision and Congressional approval to build up the shore establishment. *Courtesy of the U.S. Navy Seabee Museum.*

Workers outside the Old Steam Engineering Mechanical Shop #1, Mare Island Navy Yard, 1906. *Courtesy of the National Archives.*

U.S. Navy submarines in port, c. 1918, possibly at the New London Submarine Base, Groton, Connecticut. The submarine on the left is either USS *H-1* or USS *H-2*. The submarine in the middle is the USS *G-1*, and the one on the right is unidentified. *Courtesy of the Naval History and Heritage Command.*

General storehouse Building Number 149 at the Boston Navy Yard, built by W. Evatt Construction Company, January 3, 1918. At the outbreak of war, the need for storage space exceeded that available, necessitating additional facilities to provide for the storage of shipbuilding supplies and general industrial activities. *Courtesy of the U.S. Navy Seabee Museum.*

Members of the Public Works Department stand outside their offices at the Guam Naval Station, c. 1924. At the end of the Spanish-American War, American troops faced the problem of ruling a newly acquired colony. Illiteracy, unsanitary conditions, and disease were some of the new issues confronting the new governor. As a result, the Navy sent a Civil Engineer Corps officer to run the Public Works Department, oversee the installation of all base utilities, and create a basic infrastructure for the new base. Initially, only one Warrant Machinist and one local staff member assisted him. *Courtesy of the U.S. Navy Seabee Museum.*

Interior of Joiner Shop Machinery, Building 66, looking east, at the Puget Sound Naval Shipyard, Washington, June 11, 1935. *Courtesy of the National Archives.*

Staff of the Construction and Repair Department, Shop 24, Washington Navy Yard, District of Columbia, 1935. *Courtesy of the U.S. Navy Seabee Museum.*

View of Shipbuilding Ways No. 341 and No. 342 from the Marine Railway at the Charleston Navy Yard, South Carolina, March 12, 1931. These shipbuilding ways with hammerhead cranes, designed to construct destroyers, were constructed at the Charleston Navy Yard during World War I. *Courtesy of the U.S. Navy Seabee Museum.*

Boiler shop crew at the Mare Island Navy Yard, 1901. The boiler equipment at each main naval station consisted of twelve 600-horsepower water tube boilers equipped with super-heaters, mechanized stokers, forced and induced draft apparatus, soot blowers, balanced draft regulators, draft gauges, and automatic flue-gas analyzers and meters. *Courtesy of the National Archives.*

Staff of the Construction and Repair Department, Washington Navy Yard, District of Columbia, c. early 1900. *Courtesy of the U.S. Navy Seabee Museum.*

Photograph of Substation #3 generator at the Puget Sound Naval Shipyard, October 24, 1914. Alternating current turbo-generators were in use for years in the majority of the navy yard power plants, but were replaced by new 1,000-kilowatt direct current turbo-generator units during World War I. *Courtesy of the U.S. Navy Seabee Museum.*

Interior view of the Boat and Joiner Shop, Building 108, at the Puget Sound Naval Shipyard, Washington, May 4, 1936.
Courtesy of the National Archives.

View of Puget Sound Naval Shipyard from Pier B showing the Machine Shop, Electrical School, and Ammunition Building, July 2, 1928. *Courtesy of the U.S. Navy Seabee Museum.*

Pier D at the Naval Submarine Base New London, Connecticut, showing decking, cables, and piping removed, August 23, 1928. At this point the stringers were 40% removed and new piles stored on decks. *Courtesy of the U.S. Navy Seabee Museum.*

View of *S-22* taken off the port quarter at the Portsmouth Navy Yard, Maine, November 21, 1929, showing newly installed marker buoy (aft), motor room escape hatch, and lifting eyes (hull sides). *Courtesy of the Naval History and Heritage Command, Rear Admiral Ridley McLean Collection.*

Photograph of a Schwartz furnace inside the base foundry at the Puget Sound Naval Shipyard, October 22, 1914. Workers at the base foundry shops produced metal castings of the materials required to maintain the fleet and operate the base. The different metals are melted to a liquid inside a furnace, poured into a cast, and then removed after it has cooled. *Courtesy of the U.S. Navy Seabee Museum.*

Workers rebuilding the reinforced concrete deck at Pier 314 at the Charleston Navy Yard, South Carolina, on April 3, 1917. USS *Sterett* (Destroyer # 27) is at right, at the end of the pier. In the center is *Floating Derrick # 22. Courtesy of the Naval History and Heritage Command.*

The San Francisco Bridge Company installs temporary platforms for pier construction at Naval Air Station Alameda, May 31, 1938. *Courtesy of the U.S. Navy Seabee Museum.*

The USS *Jason* (Collier #12) alongside Pier B at the Key West Naval Station, Florida, October 1, 1913. The motor boat *Lilla* is among the small craft in the foreground. Colliers were bulk cargo ships designed to carry coal, especially for naval use by coal-fired warships. In the late nineteenth century, wooden-hulled sailing colliers were adapted for use in voyages of exploration to the South Pacific. *Courtesy of the U.S. Navy Seabee Museum.*

View of the office staff for the Construction and Repair Department at the Washington Navy Yard, District of Columbia, 1898.
Courtesy of the Naval History and Heritage Command.

Workers install gasoline tanks at Naval Submarine Base New London, May 24, 1928.
Courtesy of the U.S. Navy Seabee Museum.

A contractor installs fender wale for Pier D at Naval Submarine Base New London, Connecticut, December 1, 1928. A wale was a piece of timber bolted horizontally along a dock, about the height of a ship, to serve as a fender. *Courtesy of the U.S. Navy Seabee Museum.*

USS *L-4*, USS *L-10*, and USS *L-1*, respectively, at the Philadelphia Navy Yard, Pennsylvania, soon after their February 1, 1919, return to the U.S. from European waters. With the defeat of the Central Powers, *L-4*, *L-10*, and *L-1* departed Portland, England, January 3, 1919, and arrived in Philadelphia February 1st. From 1919 to 1922 they operated along the Atlantic coast, experimenting with new torpedoes and undersea detection equipment. *Courtesy of the Naval History and Heritage Command.*

Photograph of the wood working shop at the Naval Submarine Base, Los Angeles, c. 1922. In 1913, a Submarine Base was established on the West Coast at San Pedro, California. By 1922, the Submarine Base's facilities were soon being shared with destroyers. The base would eventually give way to the destroyers, with the last mention of the Submarine Base at San Pedro being made in official Navy Orders in 1929, when the base had already become specialized in servicing auxiliary ships. *Courtesy of the National Archives.*

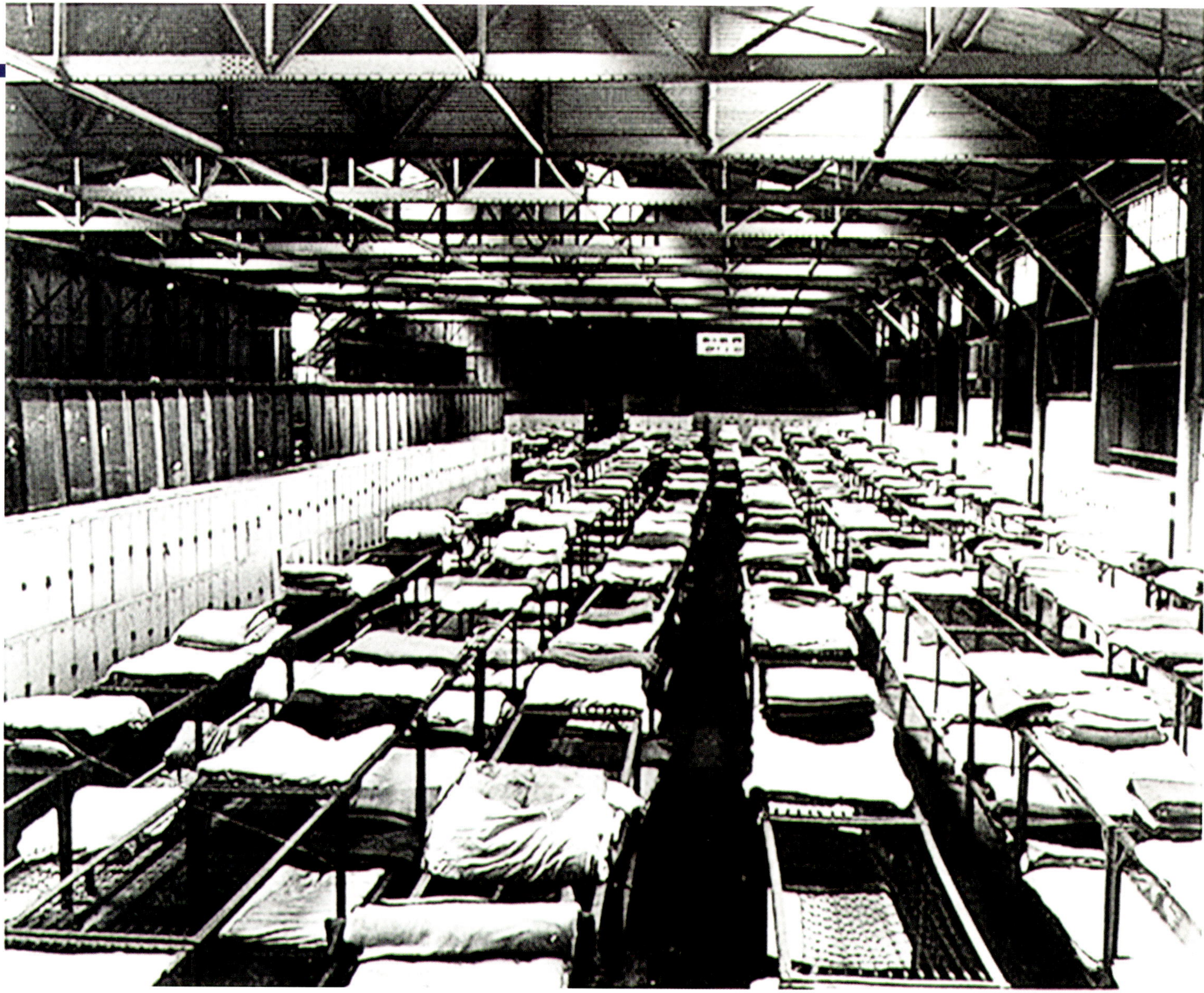

View of the enlisted sailor's double-decker bunk hall with lockers at the Naval Submarine Base San Pedro, after construction was completed in 1922. Enlisted sailors slept in rows of double-decker bunks at the newly created Naval Submarine Base in San Pedro, California. A large restroom and shower room at one end provided just enough space for the men to gather each morning. *Courtesy of the National Archives.*

USS *Shenandoah* under construction inside the Naval Air Station Lakehurst airship hangar, 1923. The USS *Shenandoah* was the first of four rigid airships built for the Navy, including the USS *Akron*, USS *Macon*, and the USS *Los Angeles*. She was built from 1922 to 1923 at the Lakehurst Naval Air Station. *Courtesy of the Naval History and Heritage Command, Collection of Admiral Thomas C. Kinkaid, USN.*

Index

Name *Page number(s)*

Name *Page number(s)*